GODS OF THE MAYA, AZTECS, AND INCAS

MYTHS OF THE WORLD

GODS OF THE MAYA, AZTECS, AND INCAS

TIMOTHY R. ROBERTS

MetroBooks

MetroBooks

AN IMPRINT OF FRIEDMAN/FAIRFAX PUBLISHERS

©1996 by Michael Friedman Publishing Group, Inc.

Library of Congress Cataloging-in-Publication data available upon request.

ISBN 1-56799-351-6

Editor: Benjamin Boyington
Art Director: Lynne Yeamans
Designer: Susan Livingston
Layout: Jonathan Gaines
Photography Editor: Deborah Bernhardt

Color separations by HBM Print Ltd.
Printed in China by Leefung-Asco Printers Ltd.

For bulk purchases and special sales, please contact:
Friedman/Fairfax Publishers
Attention: Sales Department
15 West 26th Street
New York, NY 10010
212/685-6610 FAX 212/685-1307

Visit the Friedman/Fairfax Website:
http://www.webcom.com/friedman

DEDICATION

For Iris.

ACKNOWLEDGMENTS

Special thanks to Ben Boyington for his
advice and support with this project.

CONTENTS

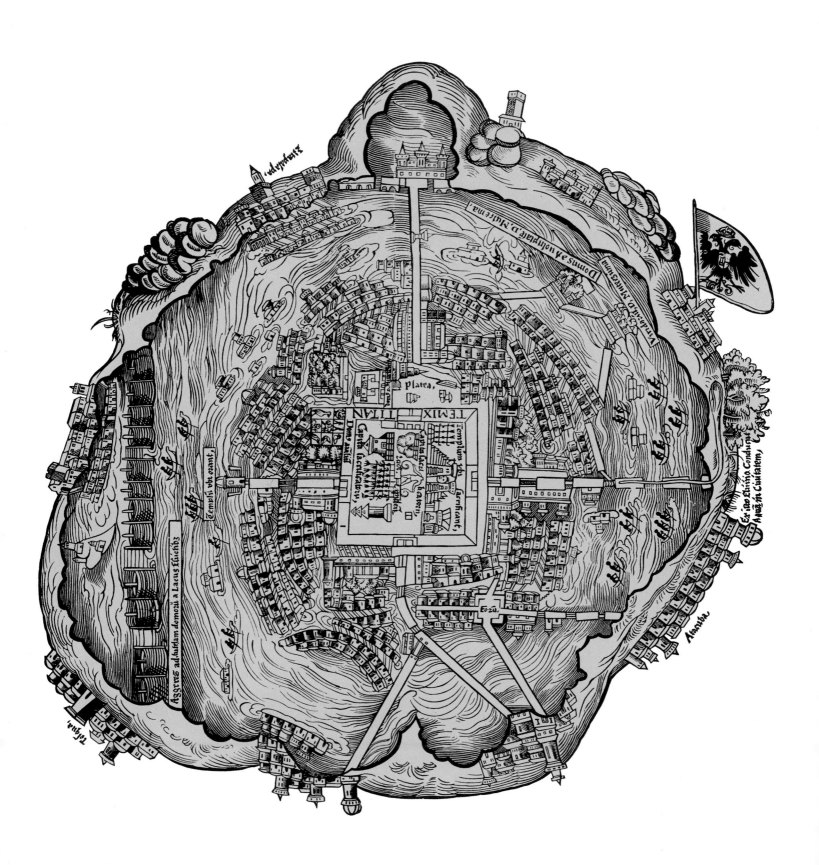

THROUGH SPANISH EYES—HOW THE MYTHS SURVIVED

When the Spanish conquistadores first discovered the great native civilizations of the New World, their faith in their own assumed superiority must have been shaken at least briefly. The cities of the Aztecs, Maya, and Incas were in many instances larger and in every instance cleaner and more orderly than the Spanish cities the conquerors had left in Spain. The native rulers seemed vastly richer than their European counterparts, and the control they exercised over their subjects was certainly more complete.

This rather fanciful map, printed in Nuremburg, Germany, in 1524, shows Tenochtitlan, drawn much larger than scale, at the center of Lake Texcoco. In the middle of the city is the great central square—the same area that stands in front of the National Cathedral of Mexico in modern-day Mexico City.

In short, the Spanish found that the societies of the New World were dynamic, growing, and progressive.

Their self-esteem shaken, the Spanish comforted themselves by claiming "moral" superiority over the natives of Central and South America—who, like their counterparts in North America, were incorrectly labeled "Indians." The invaders took comfort in collecting and circulating grisly tales of mass human sacrifices in which hundreds—or in the case of the Aztecs, thousands—of victims were butchered for the benefit of a bewildering number of gods. Few, if any, Spaniards seemed to recognize the obvious parallel with their own systematic dispatch of Jews, Moslems, and other religious nonconformists back home. And those who did make this connection certainly drew comfort from the fact that, unlike the Aztecs, the Europeans were too "civilized" to eat the people they murdered.

On the heels of the Spanish conquerors came large numbers of Catholic priests who tried to convert the Indians. This proved surprisingly easy among the non-Aztec subjects of Mexico, who resented having to provide their Aztec masters with sacrificial victims. To them, it seemed much easier to accept Spanish rule and worship a virgin with a baby than to give a certain number of their sons and daughters each year to be grilled over a brazier before having their hearts ripped out of their chests for the greater glory of Huitzilopochtli, the little green hummingbird god.

It was a little harder to convert the subjects of the Incas, who, with a few exceptions, enjoyed the order the Inca rule had provided. And hardest of all to convert were the Maya, who were divided into dozens of tribes with no central authority the Spanish could overawe, whose rulers confined their sacrifices to enemy nobles, and whose cities were protected by nearly impenetrable rain forests. Indeed the Maya conversion never really "took." To this day, the descendants of the Maya in the Yucatan still lack, somehow, a wholehearted Christian allegiance—they continue to worship at least some of their old gods, who can be disguised as various saints if the occasion warrants.

In this process of conversion, the Spanish found it useful first to learn the Indian languages and then to translate Christian Scripture into those tongues. They hoped to find within the Indian myths an element or two that they might relate to Christian belief. The Spanish friars were thrilled, for instance, when they discovered that the Maya practiced baptism of infants. To make these discoveries, however, they needed Indian informants who could describe the native religions and translate the native books—the Aztecs, who had taken the first steps toward a written language, and the Maya, who had already achieved one, had thousands of glyph books filled with pictures, myths, and legends about their gods.

In the beginning, the Spaniards were eager to listen to the informants' stories and learn about what was in the books. Once they had done this, however, most Spaniards found it easy to forget these pagan aberrations, toss the interviews aside, and burn the

Fragment of a Christian calendar written in Aztec hieroglyphics. Each rectangle represents one day of a month. For a time after the Spanish conquest, the native people in the Valley of Mexico continued using their native script. Aztecs could not write in the formal sense— they used a kind of proto-writing that was actually just an aid to memory.

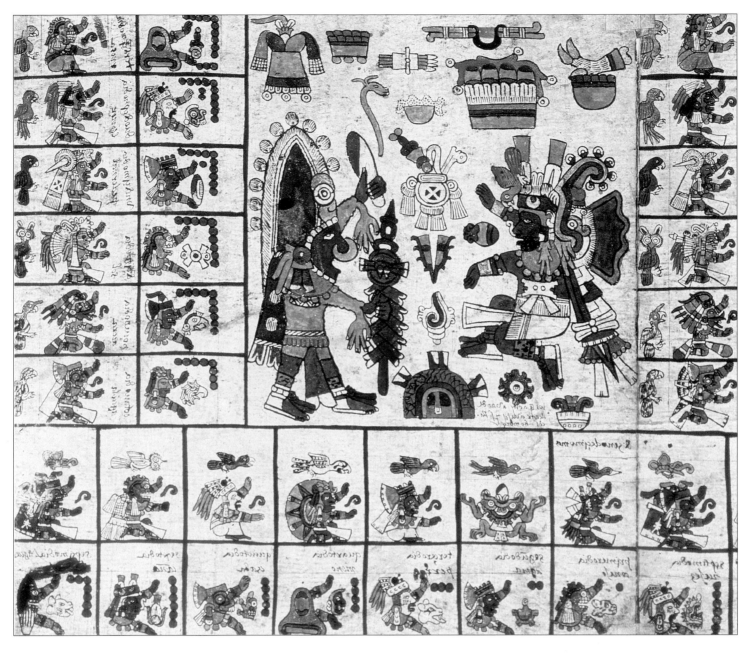

strange books—in an excess of Christian piety, thousands of original Indian manuscripts were burned. But occasionally a Spaniard who was, for whatever reason, more humane or tolerant than his fellows saw value in what he had learned or read and decided to preserve the interviews and the books. But individuals like this were rare. Out of the thousands of Indian manuscripts, only three Maya and twelve Aztec books that predated the Spanish invasion survived the literary holocaust; a few dozen transcriptions of interviews also survived. The Spaniards who made efforts to preserve these valuable records, like Bernardo de Sahagun in Mexico, Francisco de Avila in Peru, and Francisco Ximenez in Guatemala, were not, however, liberal thinkers—not by any stretch of the imagination. They were good, honest bigots with most of the prejudices and intolerances of sixteenth- and seventeenth-century Spain, but they apparently possessed some extra measure of curiosity—certainly out of step with the rest of their contemporaries—that helped them to see something valuable in the myths and legends of the Maya, Aztecs, and Incas. Today, we can only wonder at their motivation and be grateful for their eccentricities.

A page of the *Borbonicus Codex*, which was first thought to be a pre-Columbian Aztec document but is now believed to have been written around 1530. The first part of the book is a *tonalamatl*, a 260-day calendar that marks festival days. The second part is a *trecena*, a guide to predicting the future.

THE MAYA WORLD

Between about 300 B.C. and A.D. 900 the Mayan culture was the most intellectually and technologically advanced of all the five hundred American Indian groups on both continents of the Americas. During the two thousand years that span Mayan history—the last independent Mayan city was taken by the Spanish in 1697—these people made numerous architectural, mathematical, and astronomical innovations that were far ahead of the accomplishments of their New World contemporaries. Although the ancient cultures

Maya stele from Copan, Honduras, now displayed on Kukulkan Boulevard in Cancun, Mexico. Stelae were set up throughout the Maya world until about A.D. 900. Each stele honors a Maya ruler or noble and may bear inscriptions about a victory or coronation. Most have a day, month, and year inscribed on them.

Today archaeologists can read over 85 percent of the ancient Maya glyph writing. This is a small portion of a much larger stone frieze found in the ancient ruins of Ixtutz near modern-day Guatemala City. The inscription has been dated to A.D. 790.

of the Aztecs and Incas have largely disappeared, that of the Maya continues, for the modern Maya still preserve aspects of their old religion and society and still govern their lives by the ancient Mayan calendar.

The ancient Maya were also the only Indian society that had a true written language. Between 1952 and 1986, scholars from St. Petersburg, Russia, to Pittsburgh, U.S.A., have, through a massive cooperative effort, largely succeeded in translating the Maya writing. Today, scholars can read about 85 percent of all Maya inscriptions.

The Maya are also particularly noteworthy because they resisted the encroachments of the Europeans for longer than any other native group. Whereas the Aztec empire fell within two and a half years of the arrival of Cortez and the Inca resistance lasted forty years, the Maya resisted the Spaniards for 180 years, defeated three Spanish armies, and even recruited Spanish renegades to help in the Maya fight for freedom. As late as 1622, the Maya sacrificed Father Diego Delgado and his brave band of missionaries to their gods in their time-honored way atop a pyramid in the last independent Maya city, Tayasal, in northern Guatemala. It took two Spanish armies seventy-five years to reduce this last Maya stronghold.

Over the last 150 years archaeologists and historians have constructed a fairly complete picture of Maya culture, beliefs, and social structure. The Maya were a fascinating combination of the attractive and the grotesque. Some of their pyramids towered two hundred feet (61m) in the air. Their cities covered up to six square miles (15.5 sq km) of inhospitable jungle, contained nearly three thousand buildings, and had populations numbering between ten thousand and fifty thousand (although scholarly controversy rages over this point). The Maya priests charted the courses of Venus, Mars, and Mercury, devised calendars that estimated the occurrence of eclipses, and even invented the zero, with all of its wonderful implications for mathematics. Their stone masons and engineers carved beautiful reliefs and built causeways and elevated roads through jungles that give pause to modern-day engineers. The Maya also perfected an agricultural system to feed a population of millions in an area that included parts of modern Guatemala, Belize, and Mexico that today have difficulty supporting a fraction of that number. The few murals and many stone carvings that survive show a society that, at least for the nobles, emphasized beautiful surroundings, a penchant for splendid costumes, and a refined and technically advanced artistic sense.

Although the Maya had many attractive aspects and were admirable in many ways, it is no small part of the modern fascination with things Mayan that they also had a darker—indeed, truly sinister—side. They apparently reveled in war and practiced incredible cruelty on their defeated or captured enemies—common soldiers became slaves to Mayan lords, and nobles served as victims in bloody sacrificial rites. The beautifully painted and technically impressive wall murals of Bonampak, a Mayan city built in the late eighth century A.D. on the Usumacinta River in western Guatemala, depict prisoners of war with their fingernails torn out and awaiting decapitation by Mayan lords who wear severed heads, green with decay, around their necks. In these murals, noble Mayan ladies sit stoically by, poking holes in their own tongues and drawing strings through them to encourage a rich flow of blood. One noble mother holds a child on her lap as she patiently waits for another woman to pass her a knife so that she can practice this same form of mutilation on the child. We also know from various other sources that the Mayan lords were expected to draw blood not only from their tongues but also from their penises. Blood from tongues and penises was sprinkled

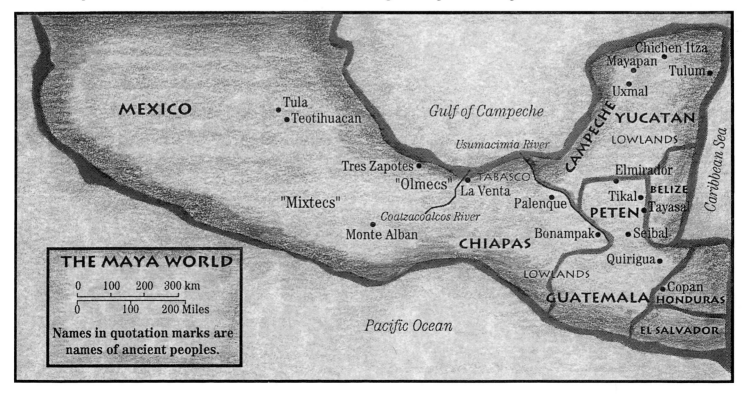

A representation of a human sacrifice atop a pyramid from the *Codex Magliabechiano*. In Mayan sacrifice, the victim was stretched backward over a stone while a priest held his feet. Meanwhile, another priest wielding a semicircular obsidian knife would make a deep incision across the chest. He would then reach in and pull the still-beating heart down and out of the chest cavity. The heart would then be placed in a sacred *quauhxicalli* (eagle's bowl) usually cut into a representation of an animal carved in stone (see illustration on page 67). Finally, the body would be rolled down the steps of the pyramid. Opinion varies among scholars as to how much of the body was eaten and by whom. This picture shows the victim's soul flying up and away from the body, followed by a trail of blood.

on bark paper that was then burned in the hope that the smoke would carry messages to the gods.

The Maya believed that their gods loved blood and human sacrifice. Later in their history, the Maya adopted the sacrificial customs of the Aztecs and sacrificed war captives by stretching them backward over a stone atop one of the great pyramids, slicing their chests open, and tearing the still-beating hearts out with their hands. The only mitigating factor for Maya apologists seems to be that the Maya did not sacrifice as many people as the Aztecs—who were reputed to have sacrificed as many as fifty thousand people a year.

Maya art does not reveal as much about the commoners as about the nobles, but when the little information it provides is combined with knowledge gleaned from archaeological investigations, we get a fairly accurate view of how the lower classes lived: their lives consisted primarily of growing the food to keep their lords fit for the hard work of war and sacrifice and serving as the "grunts" in the almost constant Mayan wars. Excavations of skeletal remains of both nobles and commoners reveal that the Mayan lords were bigger and stronger than their peasant subjects,

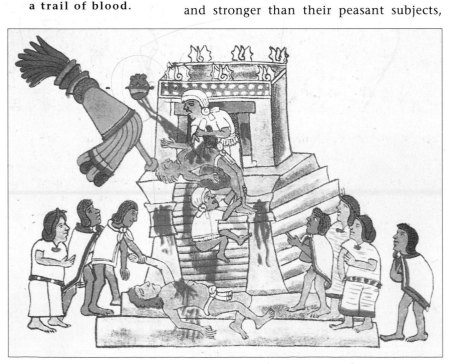

whose smaller skeletons also show many deformities—probably the result of vitamin deficiencies. Both nobles and peasants practiced the deliberate deforming of their heads. At birth, a child's head was placed between two flat boards that were joined at one end to form a 45-degree angle; the head was bound in this vise until the skull became permanently misshapen in a form the Maya apparently found appealing. Nobles and commoners alike felt that crossed eyes were

an especially attractive feature, and Maya mothers generally suspended a bead from the hair to the bridge of the nose to encourage their children's eyes to cross permanently.

But the mutilations did not end there. Both nobles and commoners slit their earlobes and then gradually expanded the cut to allow the insertion of larger and larger disks of jade, topaz, or polished wood, some of which were several inches in diameter. The Maya also punctured the sides of the nose to admit stone

decorations, plucked out their facial hair, and filed their front teeth to fine points, often inlaying them with semiprecious stones or even gold. Every possible part of the noble's body and a good portion of the commoner's, except for the breasts of the women, was covered with tattoos.

For the Mayan noblemen, the practice of mutilation also extended to the genitals: it was customary for them to slice the foreskins of their uncircumcised penises into narrow

A reproduction of a mural on the inside of the ruins at Bonampak depicting a ritual procession. The original is dated circa A.D. 800.

strips so that the tip of the organ appeared to be covered with ribbons. In their accounts of the Maya, the Spanish invaders swiftly pass over this custom, but several Spanish writers do dwell admiringly on the beauty of the Maya women, tattoos, cross-eyes, pointed heads, filed teeth, and all; admiration may, however, be a simple reflection of the length of time the conquistadores had been away from home.

To judge from the surviving murals and carvings, the Mayan elite lived in luxury. They dressed in long, spotlessly white cotton mantles, wore a great deal of jade jewelry, and decorated themselves and their clothing with the blue-green feathers of the quetzal, a beautiful Central American bird. These feathers seem to have been more valued than jade or gold, and the Maya hunted the quetzal nearly to extinction; the poor creature was saved only by the arrival of the Spanish, who discouraged the custom of wearing feathers.

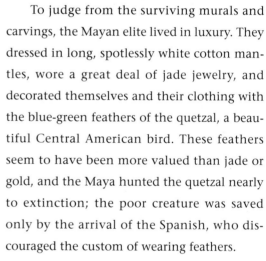

From calendar inscriptions that record the exact days of birth and death for members of the Mayan elite, we know that many of these nobles lived long lives—often well into their mid-sixties.

The main staple of the Mayan diet was maize, which was grown in *milpas*, small plots amidst the jungle growth. These plots were abandoned every two years or so to allow the soil to regain its fertility naturally. Maize by itself, however, is not a complete food because it lacks niacin and certain amino acids. To complete its nutritive capabilities, the maize must be soaked in lime to produce hominy. If maize is eaten in its natural form, it will cause pellagra, a vitamin deficiency characterized by skin problems, nerve dysfunction, hallucinations, and chronic diarrhea.

The forte of the Maya was architecture. The great cities of Tikal, Palenque, Bonampak, Uxmal, Chichen Itza, Mayapan, Copan, and Quirigua are only the best known of the ancient Mayan cities that dot the jungles of western Belize, northern Guatemala, western Honduras, and the eastern Mexican provinces of Chiapas, Campeche, Yucatan, and Tabasco. There are more than three hundred Mayan cities, with nearly two hundred awaiting detailed excavation. Most of these are ruins, many are still covered with jungle foliage, and a few have been restored. Although these cities served numerous administrative and trade needs, their main function was to serve as ceremonial centers. To facilitate the ceremonies that were essential to Mayan society, the Mayan cities had tall stone pyramids, ground-level temples, towers, and, not infrequently, structures that served as ball courts for a game that was central to Maya religion.

The pyramids, certainly the most dramatic and best-known structures of the Maya, were both tombs and temples. On the tops of these buildings, Mayan priests carried out gruesome human sacrifices to please their gods; underneath the pyramid lay the remains of the various Maya nobles who had built these structures as monuments to themselves

The great Temple of the Sun at Palenque (right) was built by the Sun Lord Chan-Bahlum (Snake Jaguar) around A.D. 683. The temple atop the pyramid has two rooms. The rear one, commonly referred to as the sanctuary, has a relief sculpture of a Jaguar God. To the left of the Sun Temple is the Temple of the Foliated Cross. There are also two other important temples at Palenque.

RIGHT: Interior of the tomb of Lord Pacal (died A.D. 683) underneath the Temple of Inscriptions at Palenque. The stone slab has been raised off the top of the sarcophagus. The tomb was discovered by Mexican archaeologist Alberto Ruz in June 1952. Ruz noted curious holes in the floor of the temple on top of the Temple of Inscriptions. These proved to be holes that allowed for the insertion of poles for raising the floor. Under the floor Ruz found the stairway leading down into the tomb.

OPPOSITE: One of the most popular reliefs found among Maya ruins are representations of ball players. While it is mainly a Maya fascination, there were also ball courts at Teotihuacan and some Aztec cities. This sculpture shows a ball player about to serve the ball with his left hand. The ball, which was rubber, measured six to twelve inches (15.2–30.5cm) in diameter. It weighed up to eight pounds. Skulls of defeated players may have been put in the center of the widest balls. On at least some occasions, the losing team was sacrificed.

and to the gods. Indeed, it appears to have been incumbent upon each succeeding lord to rebuild the various pyramids of his city—not by tearing down the old and building a new monument, but simply by building over the existing structure.

One of the most magnificent Mayan tombs lies under the great pyramid at Palenque, which is known as the Temple of Inscriptions. This tomb, which contains the body of Lord Pacal (died A.D. 683), lies fifteen feet beneath the great staircase that ascends the front of the pyramid. The tomb is accessible through a passage that starts under the floor of the temple atop the pyramid and descends eighty feet to a chamber fifteen feet below the ground surface. Along this passage excavators found six skeletons of men and women who were apparently sacrificed during Pacal's burial. The tomb chamber, which lay undisturbed for nearly thirteen hundred years before its discovery in 1952, had walls covered with paintings of the Maya underworld. The sarcophagus holding Pacal also held a fortune in jade ornaments that decorated the corpse. As

in most Mayan tombs, this one held little gold, for the Maya valued jade much more than gold.

Besides the pyramids, the most characteristic structures—at least in Mayan ruins dating from after the tenth century A.D.—were ball courts. The Mayan "game" *pokatok* was not a game played for entertainment, but a religious ceremony commemorating the mythological game played by the Mayan heroes Hunahpu and Xbalanque against the gods of the Mayan underworld. Players wore elaborate costumes that doubled as protective gear covering arms, legs, and heads. The object of the game was to drive a six-inch (15.2cm) rubber ball called an *ulli* through a stone hoop projecting vertically from the stone walls on either side of the ball court. The difficulty of the game was that players could strike the ball only with elbows or hips. For the hip shots, players wore on their hips wooden devices that projected six or seven inches (15–17.5cm) out from either side. According to Spanish chroniclers, spectators bet huge amounts on the outcome, but the game was played in deadly earnest, for the losing team was sacrificed to the gods by being decapitated. It seems no coincidence that *hom*, the Mayan word for "ball court," also means "graveyard."

HOW HUNAHPU AND XBALANQUE DEFEATED THE LORDS OF THE UNDERWORLD

Pokatok was one of the central elements of Mayan religion and myth, to judge from the number of ball courts in Mayan cities and the numerous references to the game in sculpture,

A ball goal from the ball court (*hom*) at Chichen Itza. The vertical goal set on the wall of a court probably symbolized the entrance to Xibalba—the Maya underworld.

painted designs, and their helmets were so strong that the men never suffered any injury even in the roughest games. They were so skilled with the yokes they wore around their waists that they became famous throughout the land for their ability to make the most difficult hip shots. The two men never lost a game, and people came from miles around to watch them play.

Unfortunately, like many people who possess great skill in an endeavor, One Hunahpu and Seven Hunahpu aroused great envy in those who were less skilled. The most envious of the envious were the fourteen dread lords of Xibalba, the Maya underworld. Time and time again they ascended to the world to watch the two men practice. This was easy because One Hunahpu and Seven Hunahpu's favorite hom was directly above the great hall of Xibalba, where the lords of the underworld lived. The leaders of these gods were named One Death and Seven Death, and with their twelve evil accomplices, they accounted for most of the misery of mankind. Bleeder and Pus Master reveled in infected, gangrenous wounds. Jaundice Master, Blood Gatherer, Body Sweller, Sudden Death, and Vomit Master controlled the diseases of mankind. Bone Breaker and his brothers Skull Smasher and Stab Master oversaw the wounding of warriors. And Starvation and Trash Master encouraged death among mankind through lack of food and the diseases found in rotting refuse.

After watching an especially impressive display by the two brothers, One Death said to Seven Death, "We should invite these two showoffs to play ball with us." But Bleeder, who overheard this, said, "No! Those two are so good that it would be impossible even for us gods to beat them. Let us invite them to play ball, but then trick them into violating our rules of etiquette, and kill them. Nobody will blame us then." All of the dread lords

painting, and literature. The *Popul Vuh*, a transcription of a now lost Mayan glyph book from southern Guatemala, records the details of this central mythological event.

In earliest times the god of marriage, Xpiyacoc, and his wife, Xmucane, the goddess of childbirth, had two sons named One Hunahpu and Seven Hunahpu. Both men were mighty warriors, but their favorite pastime was playing pokatok. They had the finest equipment—their arm and leg guards were of the strongest wood, decorated with cleverly agreed that this was a good plan, and they sent the brothers an invitation to visit them in the underworld.

The lords dispatched their most prestigious messengers: Shooting Owl, One-Legged Owl, Macaw Owl, and Skull Owl, who was especially fearsome—he had a head and wings, but no body. One Hunahpu and Seven Hunahpu were suitably impressed by the messengers and accepted the invitation to play ball. The unsuspecting brothers quickly ran home to tell their mother, Xmucane, and the two sons of One Hunahpu, One Monkey and One Artisan. Xmucane suspected the worst and begged her sons not to go, but the young men laughed and quickly left for the journey.

The journey to Xibalba was filled with danger—the brothers had to make three perilous river crossings. The first river was filled with blood, the second with pus, and the third with sharp spikes, but the brothers successfully negotiated crossings by using their blowguns to pole-vault over the rivers. After crossing the third river, One Hunahpu and Seven Hunahpu came to the entrance to the hall of Xibalba. Inside sat the fourteen lords, seven along each wall, and here the brothers made a fatal violation of etiquette when they greeted the lords. As they entered the hall, they failed to notice that the lords they thought were One Death and Seven Death were really wooden manikins made to resemble those gods.

Even though the brothers sealed their fate by paying homage to the dummies, the lords decided to embarrass them further before killing them. First they invited the brothers to sit on chairs that were really hot rocks that burned the young men badly. Then they sent the brothers to pass the night in the House of Utter Darkness. Before they went inside, Pus Master gave One Hunahpu and Seven Hunahpu a torch and two cigars but told the brothers that they must return these things

unused in the morning. Once the men were inside the House of Utter Darkness, it was as if they were struck blind. And to add to their distress, the place was filled with evil scrapings that sounded like the slitherings of huge, fearsome monsters. The brothers became frightened and, fearing attack, they lit the torch. But they saw nothing, and when the torch burned out, the strange sounds returned. Thinking that it was the light that had kept the monsters at bay, they quickly lit one of the cigars to gain a meager light from its glowing end. Again the sounds stopped, only

The Olmec Rain Baby—a stylized depiction of the Jaguar God. The Olmecs were the strongest cultural influence on the Mexican Isthmus from about 1200 to 800 B.C. Interestingly, their sculptures seem to record Asiatic and African features, leading to much speculation about transoceanic voyages before Columbus.

to start up again when the cigar burned out. They quickly lit the last cigar and again the slithering and bumping sounds stopped. But just as this last cigar burned out, the underworld dawn broke and the Xibalban lords opened the door. They pretended to be outraged that the torch and cigars were gone, even though they themselves had caused the noises that had scared the brothers throughout the night. The evil gods then struck off the heads of One Hunahpu and Seven Hunahpu and placed the heads in a tree outside the great hall where they could gloat over them. Then the lords stripped the bodies of their ball-playing gear and sent it back to Xmucane as a taunt. The poor woman carefully cleaned the equipment and hid it in the rafters of her house.

Meanwhile, back in the underworld, something wonderful happened. The head of One Hunahpu miraculously changed into a calabash gourd. Indeed, the whole tree was soon covered with these gourds, and the Xibalban lords came to marvel.

Afterward, the gods went home and told their families about this strange tree but forbade them to go and look at it. The daughter of Blood Gatherer, whose name was Blood Girl, was not only very beautiful but also extremely rebellious, and when she was told that she was not allowed to go and see the calabash tree, she only wanted to see it more. Late one night, she sneaked down to look at it. As she stood under the tree, the calabash gourd that had once been One Hunahpu's head spoke to her: "Maiden, they say that my juice is very sweet. Stick out your hand and I will drip some juice on it so that you may judge for yourself." The girl held out her hand, the juice dribbled into her palm, and she raised her hand to her mouth and licked it. The juice was not especially sweet—in fact, it was downright bitter—and she knew she had been tricked, but she could not make the gourd tell her why, no matter how many times she asked.

Before long, however, Blood Girl realized how the gourd had tricked her, for the drop of juice that she had tasted made her pregnant. At first she tried to conceal her condition, but as the months passed it became impossible to hide. When Blood Gatherer no-

ticed her growing belly, he demanded to know who the father was. When she honestly replied, "No one," Blood Gatherer grew angry and ordered his men to take her to the forests, kill her, and bring back her heart as proof. But Blood Girl pleaded with the men, who, bewitched by her beauty, agreed not to kill her if she could suggest a substitute for her heart. Thinking quickly, Blood Girl remembered that the sap of the croton tree was thick and red. She asked the men to take a handful of sap, shape it into a heart, and take that back to her father, which they agreed to do.

With that, poor Blood Girl had nowhere to go but to the mother of One Hunahpu and Seven Hunahpu. At first Xmucane did not want to believe Blood Girl's story, but in the end the old woman decided to let the girl stay

with her, at least until the delivery. It was not a happy confinement, however, for One Hunahpu had left two sons, One Monkey and One Artisan, at home when he left for Xibalba, and Xmucane felt that she owed more to these two boys, whom she knew were her grandchildren, than to the baby in Blood Girl's belly, who might be her grandchild.

Of course, all this changed with the birth of Blood Girl's twins, who looked so much like One Hunahpu that the old woman could no longer doubt the girl's story. Xmucane still favored One Monkey and One Artisan, for she did not like Blood Girl very much, but at least mother and children had a home. Blood Girl named one of her sons Hunahpu, after his father, and the other Xbalanque, a corruption of Xibalba, where One Hunahpu had been killed, so that neither of the boys would ever forget their father's treacherous murder at the hands of the lords of the underworld. Secretly, Blood Girl hoped for revenge against her father and the other lords of the underworld, but at the same time she feared that these same lords might someday discover that One Hunahpu had sons by the daughter of Blood Gatherer and kill them.

The two boys grew up to be strong and clever, which was fortunate because their half-brothers, One Monkey and One Artisan, were jealous and went out of their way to make the young twins' lives difficult, stealing their dinners and claiming as their own the rabbits and birds that Hunahpu and Xbalanque killed with their blowguns. But this persecution only helped the twins to develop guile and cleverness, until finally they were able to trap their half brothers in a tall tree and turn them into monkeys.

In their youth, Hunahpu and Xbalanque became experts with the blowgun, learned to communicate with animals, and became adept at magic. Once, when their grandmother ordered them to clear a field on a

OPPOSITE: A ball player statue found on the island of Jaina, which is located off the coast of Campeche and was used as a cemetery by some of the ancient Maya nobility of the region. The statue shows thick pads that circled a player above the hips. A player also wore knee pads and other protective clothing. The sculpture has been dated to A.D. 600–900.

LEFT: A stone carving from Palenque's central plaza.

The rich maize fields of Guatemala provided the staple food crop for the Maya. The discovery, cultivation, and properties of maize play a large part in Maya mythology.

Hunahpu found a rat eating maize in the field. He grabbed the rat and held the poor animal over a fire until the hair on its tail had been burned away (which, by the way, is how the rat came to have a hairless tail). The rat begged for mercy, promising to tell Hunahpu about his father if the boy let him live. Hunahpu released the rodent, and the little animal recounted the whole sorry business of how the lords of Xibalba had lured One Hunahpu and Seven Hunahpu to the underworld and killed them. The rat also told Hunahpu that their grandmother had hidden the ball-playing gear in the rafters of her house. After Hunahpu told his brother, the boys vowed to avenge their father and uncle, then quickly returned home, found the gear, and began to practice—on the same hom where their father had practiced. It was not surprising that their loud and boisterous play disturbed the lords of the underworld, who decided to get rid of the sons, as they had earlier destroyed One Hunahpu and Seven Hunahpu.

The dark gods sent an invitation to the twins to come and play ball with them, but as an insult they used the lowly louse as a messenger. On the way to deliver the message, the louse was swallowed by a toad, which was in turn swallowed by a snake, which was then swallowed by a falcon. When the bird flew over the ball court where the boys were playing, Hunahpu and Xbalanque wounded it with a blowgun dart and forced it to vomit up the snake, which vomited up the toad, which then disgorged the louse, which finally recited the invitation to play pokatok. The two boys accepted the challenge and ran off to their grandmother's house to gather their equipment. Not surprisingly, Xmucane tried—unsuccessfully—to discourage them. Though they ignored her entreaties, the boys left their protective grandmother a means of knowing how their enterprise in the underworld was going: they planted a stalk of maize in her at-

mountainside, they bewitched their mattocks and axes to work without human hands, so that they could hunt instead of working. They asked a turtle dove to stand watch and warn them if their grandmother approached, so that they could take up the tools and pretend to be working hard.

It was in this field that Hunahpu learned how their father had died in Xibalba. One day tic, and told her to watch it. As long as the stalk grew, they said, she would know they were still alive. But if the stalk withered, then she would know they were dead. With that, they hurried off to Xibalba.

On the long and treacherous road to the underworld, Hunahpu and Xbalanque crossed the rivers of blood, pus, and spikes in the same way that their father and Seven Hunahpu had—by using their blowguns to pole-vault over them. Before reaching the hall of the Xibalban lords, however, the brothers stopped and, using their magical influence over animals, sent a mosquito to spy for them. The little insect flew into the great hall and overheard the underworld lords laying plans for the twin's destruction. Again, they were planning to make the boys earn a condemnation of death by inadvertently violating the rules of etiquette. The lords would plant wooden manikins near the entrance, hoping the two would mistake these for real lords. They would offer the boys red-hot stone seats disguised as benches. They would offer them lodging in the House of Utter Darkness and kill them if they used up the torch and cigars

offered as lights for that dismal place. If the twins somehow survived the House of Utter Darkness, the Xibalban lords planned to lodge them in the House of Razors the next night, and if the young men survived that experience, the lords would put them in the House of Jaguars the next night. If the twins survived the night there, which seemed highly unlikely, the dread lords planned to put them in the House of the Bats. If, after all this, the boys still survived, they would make one boy play poka-tok without his head—a handicap they all felt would ensure a loss. The lords further agreed that once Hunahpu and Xbalanque were dead they would certainly not hang the heads in a calabash tree.

When the mosquito returned and told the brothers of these tricks, the clever twins took the time to think up ways to counteract each threat. They went into the jungle and

ABOVE: A relief sculpture of a Maya ball player striking the rubber ball with his hip. It is doubtful that players actually wore the great head ornaments during the game, but they did need to wear plenty of other protective gear.

LEFT: A stylized rendition of the butterfly jaguar. While rare throughout most of Central America, the butterfly jaguar is a common sculpture around Teotihuacan. The motif supposedly represents either fire or the souls of departed warriors. At Teotihuacan there are numerous ceramic incense burners made in the shape of the butterfly jaguar. Teotihuacan was old even in the time of the Aztecs, whose nobles visited the site as tourists. The numerous buildings on the site were built by an unknown people.

The jaguar throne at Uxmal, from the so-called Palace of the Governors next to the Great Pyramid. At its height Uxmal had a population of about ten thousand.

gathered a number of things, including the tail feathers of a macaw, two fireflies, some flat pieces of obsidian, a young coati, one hundred leaf cutter ants, and several dozen juicy deer bones. They also bought a large bowl in a village they passed through. Only after they had put all these things in their packs did they enter the great hall.

As the brothers came in, they ignored the two wooden manikins and greeted only the real lords, thus avoiding giving any offense. When offered seats, Hunahpu and Xbalanque politely refused, saying that they had no wish to sit on hot rocks. Surprised, the underworld lords decided to postpone the ball game until the next day. They offered the twins a night's lodging in the House of Utter Darkness, gave them a torch and two cigars, and instructed them to use these for light if they wished, but to return them unused in the morning. Once the young men were alone, Xbalanque took out the bright macaw tail feathers and stuck them on the end of the unlighted torch where their brightness illuminated the house. They also took the two fireflies and put them on the

ends of the cigars to use as light. So they spent a comfortable night and woke the next morning refreshed and ready to play ball.

On the ball court, the lords of Xibalba asked the boys if they would like to bet on the outcome of the game. Both agreed, asked what the stakes were, and were told that the losers must give the winners a bowl of flowers. The boys played hard, but lost. The lords said that they must hand over the bowl of flowers in the morning and immediately sealed the brothers in the House of Razors. That night the twins were threatened by numerous flying obsidian blades. But the young men took the flat pieces of obsidian from their packs and attached them to their arm guards and waist yokes—and with this "armor" they easily deflected the flying obsidian blades. Then they spoke to the obsidian blades: "If you stop trying to cut us, when we return to the world, we will sacrifice animals to you every year." Pleased by this offer, the obsidian blades stopped.

But the problem of how to find a bowl of flowers for the lords of the underworld still remained. And the brothers knew that if they failed, they would most certainly be slain in the morning. Then Hunahpu drew the leaf cutter ants from his bag and instructed them to go into the garden of the lords of the underworld, cut some flowers, and carry them back to the House of Razors, where he put the flowers in the bowl he had brought with him. When the lords let the brothers out in the morning, they were surprised to see them

holding the bowl of flowers. The Xibalbans mumbled and grumbled, but they knew that they had been beaten.

The second day they played ball with the Xibalbans, and the brothers won. The lords were enraged, but they held their anger in check and sent the brothers to spend the night in the House of the Jaguars. When the door shut behind Hunahpu and Xbalanque, the jaguars began to circle in toward them for

This mural from Bonampak, which dates to about A.D. 800, depicts a group of Maya nobles. The glyphs below explain that the nobles are discussing the capture of an enemy leader. The rectangles at the top were supposed to hold the men's names, but they were never filled in.

RIGHT: Although there were no spectacular ruins in the territory of present-day Costa Rica, the ancient inhabitants produced charming pottery figurines. This is a jaguar bowl from Chorotega, Costa Rica.

BELOW: The Temple of the Bats at Yaxchilan, with a young Lacandon Maya girl sitting on the great sacrificial stone that once dominated the city square. Yaxchilan is a few miles from Bonampak, the site of the famous wall murals that record the sacrifice of captives by King Chaan-muan to commemorate the elevation of his infant son to the kingship of Yaxchilan. The murals were painted around A.D. 790.

the kill. But the young men quickly pulled out the deer bones and threw them to the jaguars, who settled down to feast and ignored the boys for the rest of the night.

When the Xibalbans opened the door of the House of the Jaguars, they found a room full of sleeping cats, curled up in a circle about the brothers. Again they were shocked and frustrated that another carefully laid trap had failed. "Let us play especially well today," they said to one another, "and when we have defeated them, we will kill them." But when the game ended that day, the brothers had beaten the dread lords a second time. One Death grumbled and said, "You've been lucky. Sleep well tonight, and we will play the final game tomorrow." With that, they led the brothers to the House of the Bats and locked them in.

Now the bats that lived in this house had jaws made of obsidian, and they could slice off a head with great ease. To protect themselves, the twins used their magic to make themselves very small and crawled inside their blowguns to spend the night. But Hunahpu foolishly stuck his head out of the end of his blowgun, and a bat swooped down and cut it off. The head rolled onto the floor and one of the bats swooped down, grabbed

it, flew with it to the end of the ball court, and dropped it in the jungle. Hunahpu should have died, but he did not because the young men had defeated One Death and Seven Death again and again—twice on the ball court, twice in the great hall, and three times in the Houses of Utter Darkness, Razors, and Jaguars—and thus became immortal.

But they still could not play ball very well when Hunahpu had no head. Thinking quickly, Xbalanque pulled the little coati from his bag and said, "Go out and bring back your favorite food." The little creature ran off and soon came back with a gourd, and Xbalanque spent the rest of the night carving the gourd into a head to fit on Hunahpu's body. In the morning the Xibalban lords were again amazed to find that the twins had survived the night, but they concealed their dismay, went out to the hom, and began to play ball. Of course, Hunahpu's body did not play very well, so, as soon as he could, Xbalanque knocked the ball out of bounds in the direction where Hunahpu's real head lay and ran with Hunahpu's body to retrieve the head. In the security of the jungle, Xbalanque removed

the gourd and attached the real head, then returned with Hunahpu to finish the game, beating the Xibalban lords a third time.

Now the evil lords of the underworld were very angry. They had used every trick they could think of to defeat the brothers and had failed every time. They decided on one last trick. They built an oven, invited the two brothers to dinner, then seized the twins and threw them in. When their bodies were burned and only bones were left, the Xibalbans raked the bones out of the oven, ground them to powder, and tossed the powder into the water.

At the very moment that the young men were burned in the oven, the stalk of maize in Xmucane's attic began to wither, and the old woman grieved. But five days later, she was thrilled to see that the plant had suddenly turned green again. For the twins were immortal, and the water of the river only restored them to life. They emerged from the river fully re-formed, and began to plan their final revenge.

LEFT: A mask of carved jadite with shell and obsidian inlay for eyes. Such masks were used to cover the faces of the dead, or were set up in niches.

BELOW: A white-nosed coati. The coati ranges from southern Arizona and New Mexico to Panama. It is about the size of a raccoon, but longer. The clever coati figures often in Maya mythology.

RIGHT: Probably made between A.D. 250 and A.D. 600, this terra-cotta rendition of a warrior with an eagle headdress was used as an incense burner—the smoke came out of the mouth. Although this is a Mayan creation, it looks very similar to statues of Aztec eagle warriors made 800 years later and 700 miles (1,120km) to the west at Tenochtitlan.

Hunahpu and Xbalanque disguised themselves as wandering magicians and roamed throughout the great jungle cities. They swallowed swords, walked on stilts, and shut themselves up in burning huts, only to emerge unharmed. Their greatest trick was for one brother to sacrifice the other by striking off his head, slicing open his chest, and pulling out his heart. After a few moments, the headless, heartless corpse would leap up off the altar, grab his heart, put it back in his chest cavity, and then walk over to his head, pick it up, and put it back on.

Soon the reputation of these great magicians reached the Xibalban lords, who sent one of their owl messengers to summon the magicians to perform at Xibalba. Soon the two brothers—who were disguised so well that nobody recognized them—arrived at the great hall of the underworld and began their act. They danced, swallowed swords, and walked on stilts, but these things bored the Xilbalban lords, who asked Hunahpu and Xbalanque to perform their famous sacrifice trick. The two brothers were glad to comply. When they were finished, One Death, the coruler of Xibalba, said, "Tell me how you did that."

"It is merely a trick, great lord. I can show you how," replied Hunahpu.

"I want to learn the trick, too," said Seven Death.

The two brothers positioned the two lords of Xibalba on the sacrificial stones, cut off their heads, and pulled out their hearts. The other twelve lords of the underworld waited for the corpses to rise up, put their hearts back

in their chests, and put their heads back on their shoulders. When that did not happen, they turned to the twins for an explanation—and they got one. Hunahpu and Xbalanque faced the lords, took off their disguises, and

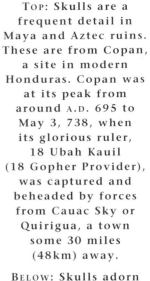

Terra-cotta relief of Kinich Ahau, the Maya Sun God. Terra-cotta sculptures were often affixed to the walls of temple-pyramids. This one is from an archaeological site at Campeche, Mexico.

said: "We have avenged our father, One Hunahpu, and his brother, Seven Hunahpu, and now we will kill you." But the twelve remaining lords of Xibalba begged for their lives, and the brothers agreed to let them live, but decreed that from that moment on none of the dread lords would ever enjoy the pleasure of having a human sacrificed to them—they would have to be content with animal and vegetable sacrifices.

To reward Hunahpu and Xbalanque, the god Itzamna, who ruled all the gods, turned Hunahpu into the Sun and Xbalanque into the Moon so that ever afterward, when people looked at the sky, they would remember the bravery and cleverness of the twins.

HOW THE GODS CREATED THE WORLD

One of the most common themes in mythology—regardless of where or when the myths come from—is the selfishness of the gods. In ancient Greek mythology, when Hades kidnapped Demeter's beautiful daughter, Persephone, Zeus refused to help his sister get the girl back until Demeter, the goddess of agriculture, condemned mankind to death by refusing to let anything on Earth grow until her daughter was returned. Finally, Zeus, selfishly fearing that with mankind gone there would be no one to worship him or his fellow Olympians, pressured Hades to release the girl, which he did.

A similar theme underlies the actions of the Mayan gods as preserved in the *Popul Vuh*, the great mythological collection of the Maya. In this book it is made clear that the gods created mankind and the earth to support them, because the gods needed creatures to worship them and make sacrifices to them.

In the earliest times, there were only three things in the universe: the sky, the sea, and the gods of the sea and sky, marriage and childbirth, fire, dawn, and mountains, and the king of the gods. The sky gods were named Sky Heart, Newborn Thunder, and Hurricane. The sea gods included Heart of the Lake, Sea Heart, and Feathered Serpent. One day, as they surveyed the universe, they complained of their loneliness and wondered what they might do about it. First they decided to make mountains, lakes, rivers, and fields. These were easy enough, for the gods merely had to think of what they wanted to create and those things would rise from the seabed perfectly formed. But when the gods

This sculpture, which is known as a *Chacmool*, is from Chichen Itza and dates to about A.D. 1000. This word, which means "red jaguar paw" in Yucatan Mayan, was coined by French archaeologist Augustus Le Plongeon. There are dozens of chacmools throughout the Maya world. The sculptures vary in detail, but they are always of a figure reclining on its elbows, its face turned at a 90-degree angle, and holding a bowl in his lap to receive offerings. The bowl is similar in function to the *quauhxicalli*, or "eagle bowls," of the Aztec that received recently extracted hearts. The Aztecs called the figures that held such bowls *cuauhxicalli*.

Maya clay figurine from Campeche, Mexico. Such figures are usually found in tombs. This one was made between A.D. 700 and 1000.

decided to make a creature to populate this new world and worship them, they found the process too complicated to achieve by thought alone; it turned out that they needed to use the elements of the earth.

First they tried to form men and women out of reeds by bending and shaping plants into humanoid form. This effort failed, how-ever, because the beings they made were un-able to talk—they could only grunt, howl, and scream. The gods did not destroy these crea-tures, the *voh*, but allowed them to run off into the forests to become animals.

Next, they determined to use mud, and carefully crafted men and women from the mud at the bottom of the sea. What they got, however, were creatures that could not move, talk, or reproduce, but who merely sat in one place and were gradually worn down by the wind and the rain. You can still see the remnants of these creatures in certain rock formations throughout the world that have a vaguely human shape.

Having failed twice, the gods felt compelled to ask the help of Xpiyacoc and his wife, Xmucane, the god and goddess, respectively, of marriage and childbirth. These two gods, who were renowned for their great wisdom, suggested that men be carved out of wood. But when the carving was finished, the creatures were again deficient, for while they could talk, move, and reproduce, they were not intelligent enough to remember how to perform the sacred ceremonies that the gods so desired. Frustrated with this third failure, and forgetting the dignity with which gods are supposed to act, the divine rulers of the sea and the sky threw a collective tantrum. They screamed and wailed and grabbed their new creations and tore them to pieces like angry children might break a toy. They ground the creature's faces in the dirt, and even animated household implements so that clay pots, tortilla griddles, and grinding stones attacked the poor wooden beings. Many were destroyed, but a few escaped by climbing high into the trees, where they survived and become monkeys.

Completely discouraged, the gods took stock of what else they could use to make people. It was then that Feathered Serpent remembered something that a clever fox had recently discovered. Under a great rock, the little animal had found a plant with yellow, white, red, and black kernels surrounded in a sheath of green leaves. This was maize, and Feathered Serpent suggested that the gods might use this plant to form humans. The gods ground the maize to a fine powder, mixed it with water, and molded the first men

A clay incense burner from Palenque. The figure is of the Sun God, but it is also the Maya hieroglyphic for the day *ik*, one of the twenty day signs that was combined with the numbers 1 to 13 to make up the 260 days of the Maya religious calendar.

and women from it. The first four men were named Jaguar Quitze, Jaguar Night, True Jaguar, and Mahucutah; the first four women were named Great Seahouse, Shrimp House, Hummingbird, and Macaw Woman.

At first, the gods were pleased—the new creatures were intelligent, could remember all the complicated rituals of worship, and were beautiful to look at. Unfortunately, they had one drawback: they were too curious. Almost as soon as they were created, they started to ask questions about the gods: Why did they demand worship in a particular way? How had the gods created them? And why did humans have to worship the gods at all? These people were so full of questions that the gods, who were selfish when it came to sharing their knowledge, began to worry that humans might learn all the secrets of the universe and so become as wise as the gods themselves. To protect their privileged position, the gods caused a cloud to fall over the minds of humankind so that men and women could never have perfect knowledge of the world and, being unable to explain all its mysteries, would turn to the gods for answers.

For a long time, the humans were content to live and multiply, and in a short time the world became filled with their offspring. In

A relief of Yaxum Balam piercing his penis while his wife pierces her tongue. Blood letting was a requirement of the Maya nobility, with men concentrating their attentions of the penis and women drawing blood exclusively from the tongue. The relief is from Yaxchilan.

time, however, Jaguar Quitze, Jaguar Night, True Jaguar, and Mahucutah began to ask each other questions about the world, and, when they could find no answers among themselves, they decided to ask the gods. One of the first things they wanted to know was why the earth was so dark and why it was so cold. The gods told the four men that if they wanted light and warmth, they needed fire and the sun, and that these wonderful things could be found far to the west at a place called Tulan Zuyna, or the Place of the Seven Caves. Tulan Zuyna was where Itzamna, king of all the gods, lived, along with Tohil, the god of fire; Auilix, the god of the dawn; and Hacauitz, the god of the mountains. If Jaguar Quitze, Jaguar Night, Mahucutah, and True Jaguar wanted to travel to Tulan Zuyna, they could ask the gods who lived there for the gifts of fire and the sun. The men set out immediately, and after a long journey, they reached Tulan Zuyna, where they petitioned Itzamna for a sun and Tohil for fire. Tohil gave them fire on condition that they take him, Auilix, and Hacauitz back home to be worshiped. Itzamna was angry that Tohil, Auilix, and Hacauitz wanted to leave him alone at Tulan Zuyna, but he said nothing about this and told the men that the sun would appear when they reached home. Tohil gave the men a small pot with fire in it and a litter on which to carry him and his fellow deities. To thank the gods, the four men drew blood from their tongues and penises, splattered it on pieces of bark paper, and burned the bark in a sacrificial fire. Then, rejoicing, they began the journey home.

Unfortunately, during the journey, a thunderstorm arose and the rain put out the fire in the pot. The travelers were panic-stricken, and they prayed to Tohil to give them more fire. Tohil agreed, even promising to teach them how to make fire if they in turn promised to sacrifice human hearts to him

ever after. When the four men agreed, Tohil stooped, untied his sandal strap, and twirled on his heel. From the friction came fire. He also told them how to make fire by using an obsidian mirror to concentrate the rays of the sun onto tinder.

When they returned home, the sun appeared in the sky as promised, but Itzamna then took revenge on the gods who had abandoned him—as soon as the sun's rays shone on Tohil, Auilix, and Hacauitz, the three gods were turned to stone. The people were horri-

A war chief on the south wall of Room One at Bonampak. He is resplendent in his quetzal feathers. Dated to about A.D. 800.

fied, for it seemed that their gods were now powerless. The four leaders prayed to the divines and discovered that although the gods could not move, they could still speak to humans with their minds. Tohil told the humans that they must now sacrifice many human hearts to try and return the three gods to their former selves. Desperate to save their gods, the men began hunting down people to sacrifice. They spared only the members of their immediate families, waylaying other people in the jungle (the Maya sources don't explain these people's origins) and sacrificing them on the spot, cutting off their heads and tearing their hearts from their chests.

When these horribly mutilated bodies were first discovered in the jungle, people thought the murders were the work of wild animals, but they quickly learned the true story and plotted to destroy the three gods and the people who were really responsible. They sent armies against the place where the gods were hidden, but the gods confused their enemies with mists, rain, earthquakes, and other natural forces—and the statues of Tohil, Auilix, and Hacauitz were never found.

When three attempts to find and destroy the gods with armed groups of men had failed, the people tried trickery. Instead of armies, they sent two beautiful maidens named Xtah and Xpuch to discover where the gods were hidden. But Tohil, Auilix, and Hacauitz foiled this attempt by sending out spirit forms of themselves that looked like three handsome boys. The maidens and the spirit boys met on a river bank. The girls, thinking that the boys might know where the gods were, tried to seduce the boys. Being gods, however, the boys were able to resist the maidens' charms, and they played a trick on the girls.

The three boys gave each of the girls a beautiful cloak with quetzal feathers on the outside and a rich red lining painted with realistic wasps on the inside. "Take these cloaks to your chiefs," they said. When Xtah and Xpuch gave the cloaks to their leaders, the men were impressed and immediately threw the cloaks around their shoulders. Suddenly, the pictures of wasps inside the cloaks came to life and stung the men to death.

With this, the people's anger grew to even greater heights. First, they punished Xtah and Xpuch for foolishly bringing the cloaks back by condemning them to become the world's first prostitutes. Then the people selected new leaders who decided that instead of trying to find the hiding place of the three gods, they should seek out and kill all the followers of Jaguar Quitze, Jaguar Night, Mahucutah, and True Jaguar.

These new leaders gathered a huge army and marched toward the city where the four former leaders and their followers lived. But as this force—which heavily outnumbered the defenders of the gods—drew near to the city, the defenders threw bags filled with wasps over the walls. These insects stung the attackers so badly that they lost heart and retreated. Then Jaguar Quitze and his three compatriots led a counterattack, which was so successful that the weakened and demoralized attackers were forced to make peace and agree to provide a yearly tribute of human sacrifices to the three gods.

Although it may seem strange that victory should go to those who sacrificed their fellow humans and those who tried to stop this cruelty met with defeat, we must remember that human sacrifice was considered a necessity for the welfare of Indian civilizations throughout Mesoamerica, and abolishing the sacrifices would have seemed a great evil. The descendants of the Maya continued human sacrifices until 1868, when Mexican authorities reported that some isolated groups of Maya in the back country of Chiapas continued the brutal sacrificial rites.

The Maya maize god.
A stylized ear of
corn sprouts from his
head and he wears a
skull around his neck.
In Aztec society
the maize deity is
usually the goddess
Chicomecoatl.

Harvested maize. The life-blood of Maya and Aztec society, this plant has been cultivated in Mesoamerica from at least 2000 B.C.

HOW MAIZE CAME INTO THE WORLD

When humans were first created, there was no maize, and the people lived by eating roots and fruits from the trees and by hunting. The only corn in the world grew under a great rock in a crevice so deep and narrow that only the ants could reach it. Day after day the tiny ants went down the cracks in the rocks and brought up kernels of corn to take back to their ant hills.

There came a day, however, when a clever red fox noticed the juicy kernel that an ant was carrying and took it from the insect. The fox was so pleased with the flavor of this kernel that he spent the rest of the day happily taking corn away from the ants and eating it. When the sun went down, he returned to his den to sleep. During the night he passed gas and the rest of the foxes noticed the pleasant, sweet smell.

"What have you been eating to make such good smells?" asked the leader of the foxes.

Not wanting to share his secret, the fox who had discovered the corn claimed that he had only eaten some wild honey.

"It certainly doesn't smell like a honey fart to me," said the leader, but let the matter drop, and decided that he would keep an eye on this lying fox.

The next day, when the foxes scattered to search for food, the fox leader and some friends followed the first fox through the forests. They saw him stop by a trail near a big rock and take maize kernels from the ants as they emerged from a crack in the rock. They jumped out and confronted the sneaky fox, and he admitted that he had been eating what the ants had been bringing up from beneath the earth. Then all the foxes settled down to hijacking the corn that the ants were bringing up from under the rock.

But ants are not totally stupid, and when they realized that the foxes would continue eating their maize, they stopped bringing it out of the crack. The foxes begged the ants to continue bringing out the corn, but the insects refused. "Why should we work for you?" they said, and left to search for other food.

The foxes, who by now liked maize better than any food they had ever tasted, sat down to discuss what to do. One suggested that they ask the rat to go down the hole to get the corn, but another said that the rat was probably too big to fit in the crack to the corn and, besides, he was a greedy beast who would most likely take all the corn for himself and his huge family.

The foxes were silent for awhile, until the one who had found the maize in the first place said: "Let us ask Yaluk, the chief of the lightning gods, to help us. He can send a lightning bolt to crack the rock open and then we can get the maize easily."

Everyone agreed that was a good idea, and the foxes sent a messenger to Yaluk. But Yaluk was old and refused to come, even when the messenger fox described how good the maize tasted. The fox was about to leave the great hall of Yaluk when two lesser gods, Cakulha, who rules lesser lightning bolts, and his brother Coyopa, who rules the sound of thunder, told the fox that they would help.

Cakulha, Coyopa, and the fox returned to the great rock, and the two gods cast a lightning bolt at the rock. There was a great crash, but the rock did not break open. They tried again, and still nothing happened. The two gods grew angry and hurled lightning bolt after lightning bolt at the rock. The world shook with the sound, and all the gods awakened and became angry.

None was angrier than Yaluk. Disappointed with the performance of his fellow gods of lightning, he strode to the place where they were hurling their ineffective bolts. He surveyed the site and said in a loud voice: "You are fools! You throw bolts against the

rock without thinking. You need to combine wisdom with strength."

Then he called the woodpecker and said, "Tap your beak against the rock to find where the rock is weakest."

The little bird did just that. He tapped all over the rock until the tone of his tapping changed, indicating the thinnest part of the rock. The woodpecker showed the spot to Yaluk, who threw a lightning bolt against that spot and split the rock wide open. The great explosion sent particles of rock flying all over the place and a small particle of rock hit the woodpecker's head and caused blood to flow, coloring the top of the bird's head red, which is why today the woodpecker has a red head. But the little bird felt that this was a small price to pay for freeing this delicious food from the earth so that all creatures could enjoy it. This is why today, throughout Guatemala and southern Mexico, the woodpecker is regarded as a sign of good fortune and prosperity for all who see him.

According to Maya legend, the reed on a woodpecker's head is the result of a chunk of rock that hit the poor bird when the lightning god Yaluk split open the boulder under which the world's first maize plant grew. Because of its association with the discovery of maize, the woodpecker is regarded throughout Latin America as a sign of good luck. Almost all pre-Columban inhabitants of America regard the woodpecker as a good omen.

II

THE AZTEC WORLD

Thanks to the combined efforts of archaeologists, historians, and linguists, we have a clearer picture of the origins, customs, and development of the Aztecs than of any Indian civilization in Central or South America. Linguists, for instance, have discovered that the Aztec language is related to the Shoshone-Paiute language family of the Great Basin area in present-day Nevada. This is entirely consistent with Aztec legends, in which it is said that these people left their original homeland "far to the north" in A.D. 1090.

In the center of Mexico City, in front of the National Cathedral, are the excavated bases of the pyramids of Huitzilopochtli and Tlaloc. Together, these temples are often referred to by archaeologists as the Templo Mayor.

The great Sun Temple of Teotihuacan. Teotihuacan was an active city for six hundred years—from A.D. 1 to 600. The Aztecs, who saw this city only as a ruin, revered it as the birthplace of the gods. According to some accounts, there are seven caves under the pyramid that legend claims as the birthplace of either humanity or the gods—depending on the legend. The ruins of this great city cover six square miles (15.5 sq km).

By 1168, the Aztecs had migrated to the edge of the great Valley of Mexico, a three-thousand-square-mile (7,770 sq km) basin surrounded by mountain peaks. In the center of this valley was a great lake around which civilizations had flourished for centuries. The Aztecs were barbarian invaders who were initially out of place in this ancient, sophisticated world. Thirty miles (48km) to the northeast of this lake, upon which the Aztecs would eventually build their capital city of Tenochtitlan, the barbaric invaders found the deserted ruins of the city Teotihuacan. By the time the Aztecs discovered it, this huge city of temples was already six hundred years old; its main feature was the Temple of the Sun, which was 213 feet (64.9m) high with a base that covered ten acres (4ha).

Concurrent with the arrival of the Aztecs was the collapse—which they, in fact, probably contributed to—of the Toltec civilization centered at Tula, some sixty miles (96km) north of the lake. The fall of the Toltecs left a political vacuum in which twenty little city-states scattered around the shores of the great lake struggled for power, with four cities—Azcapotzalco, Colhuacan, Texcoco, and Xaltocan—being the major contenders.

The Aztecs quickly found employment as mercenaries for the Tepanacs who ruled Azcapotzalco on the lake's western edge. Their employers were so impressed with the Aztecs' fighting ability that they gave the mercenaries land on their southern frontier, near the great springs called Chapultepec. From there, the newcomers launched raids against the city of Colhuacan. Around 1298, however, these raids became such a problem for the Colhuas that they mobilized a huge army and mauled the badly outnumbered Aztecs, dragging them off to be serfs and cultivate their floating maize plots known as *chinampas*. The chinampas—clever inventions designed to prevent invaders from gaining access to their source of food—were carefully maintained plots of rich soil, each of which had been transported from the mainland and enclosed in what can only be described as a huge basket that floated on the lake's surface.

The Aztecs, however, were not content as serfs. In 1322 they picked a fight with the Colhuas by sacrificing a Colhua princess to Huitzilopochtli, their green hummingbird god; they were then forced to flee to two low and swampy islands just off the western shore of the lake. The Colhuas did not follow—they knew that the islands were easy to defend and were full of rattlesnakes, which they hoped would finish off the Aztecs. A few years later, a group of traders visited the islands and found that the snakes were gone—the Aztecs had eaten them all.

The ancient city of Tula lies fifty miles (80km) north of Tenochtitlan. Tula continued the culture of Teotihuacan after that city fell around A.D. 600. Tula became a center for the Toltec Empire from A.D. 968–1168. In 1168, however, the city was conquered by the Chichimecs, or "sons of dogs," who invaded from the north. The fifteen-foot (4.6m) stone pillars shown here once supported the roof of the temple of Quetzalcoatl, who was the chief Toltec god.

A giant rattlesnake god found in the excavations of the temple of Huitzilopochtli in the central plaza of Mexico City. Rattlesnakes are a favorite artistic rendition of the Aztecs. The fierce goddess Coatlique, the mother of Huitzilopochtli, is often represented by a statue composed entirely of rattlesnakes. Her head, for instance, is in fact two rattler heads turned sideways and facing each other so that the sides of their mouths and the eye of each snake forms a face.

For the next hundred years, the Aztecs entered into various murderous military and political activities around the lake. During this period, the Aztecs once again became mercenaries for the Tepanecs and helped them to conquer Texcoco, a city on the eastern edge of the lake.

As the city-state Azcapotzalco grew in power and prestige so did the fortunes of its Aztec mercenaries. On their two islands, the new residents built two cities. On the southern island they built Tenochtitlan, which means "Place of the Prickly Pear Cactus," as well as an earthen pyramid dedicated to Huitzilopochtli. On the northern island they built another pyramid sacred to Huitzilopochtli, and a city named Tlatelolco, or "Place of the Mounds." In a short time, the populations of the two islands grew so large that the people of both had to build out into the channel separating them. Soon, the two islands merged into one. Today, the ruins of the pyramid of Tlatelolco lie under the Square of Santiago in modern Mexico City, while the ruins of the great pyramid of Tenochtitlan can be found beneath the *Zocalo*, or main plaza, of the city.

Another sign of progress was the gradual change from buildings of adobe to structures of stone. The towns lacked only one thing in abundance—water. When the population of the islands became too large, it became necessary to find a new source. To the west, on the coast, were the great springs of Chapultepec, where the Aztecs had once lived, but these were under the control of Azcapotzalco. By coincidence, at the same time that the Aztecs began to fear they might outgrow their water supply, Maxtla, the Tepanec ruler of Azcapotzalco, was beginning to fear that soon the Aztecs would outgrow the ability of Azcapotzalco to control them. He therefore engineered the assassination of the Aztec king, Chimalpopoca, hoping to install a less ambitious king. Instead the Aztecs elected a new king, Itzcoatl, or Obsidian Serpent, who organized the Aztecs for a war of revenge. Itzcoatl, who ruled the Aztecs from 1427 to 1440, began the great orgy of conquest that was to end only with the arrival of the Spaniards in 1519.

Itzcoatl was a skilled diplomat but not a particularly skillful soldier. Aware of his military shortcomings, he appointed one of his nephews, Tlacaellel, to be commander in chief. The new general, who went on to command the Aztec armies for the next sixty-nine years(!), was a fascinating combination of brilliance and psychosis. His strategies almost always brought victory, and under him the Aztec rule grew to include all of central Mexico from the Pacific Ocean to the Gulf of Mexico. He also seems to have taken extraordinary measures to eliminate dangerous enemies beyond those involved in the normal, contemporary politics in the Valley of Mexico and to have genuinely reveled in cruelty, mutilation, and mass murder. The huge gory spectacles that so disgusted the Spanish seem to have been his invention. Although human sacrifice in the form of tearing a victim's heart from his body was a normal part of pre-Aztec Mexico, Tlacaellel increased the extent and brutality of the practice. In 1487, to celebrate the dedication of the new temple of Huitzilopochtli in Tenochtitlan, he ordered the sacrifice of eighty thousand victims in four days. In addition, he decreed that every town throughout the empire would hold sacrifices every three months. Besides these big sacrifices, there were numerous intermittent ceremonies.

Woodrow Borah, an authority on the demographics of pre-Columbian Mexico, estimates that the Aztecs sacrificed 250,000 victims every year. Other authorities put the figure at fifty thousand—still an imposing number.

Undoubtedly, these excessive sacrifices served a political purpose: already subjugated towns were scared into remaining loyal and towns outside Aztec control were thus encouraged to come into the fold or face unparalleled brutality. When Chalco, a town at the southern end of the great lake, refused an invitation to join the Aztec Empire, Tlacaellel

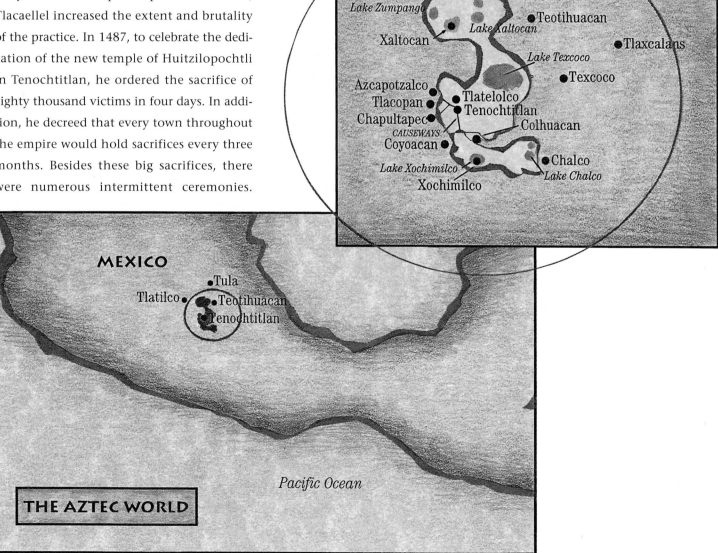

THE AZTEC WORLD

took five hundred prisoners and created a new type of sacrifice for them—the fire sacrifice. He ordered a huge brazier built at the base of Huitzilopochtli's pyramid, then had the Chalcoque prisoners tossed onto the hot coals to char before being pulled out—still living—to have their hearts torn from their bodies.

The sacrifice of Tlacaxipehualiztli—the Skinning Rite—was another favorite of Tlacaellel. In this rite, a captured warrior was tied by the waist to a stone wheel and forced to fight four Aztec warriors armed with obsidian swords. The prisoner himself had only a sword edged with feathers. When the victim was no longer able to fight because he was either wounded or exhausted, his heart was torn out and he was skinned. Specially selected Aztec warriors then wore the skin and danced around the city for twenty days, peri-

odically entering houses where they were given rich gifts. At the end of this period, the skin, now putrefying, was buried in an elaborate ceremony.

Tlacaellel made the taking of victims an end in itself. Warriors fought, not to kill their enemies, but to capture them. For an Aztec warrior, advancement through the ranks was dependent on the number of victims captured, and his costume reflected the number of sacrificial victims he had brought home. Failure to capture victims could, over time, result in demotion to a lower class. A nobleman, or *pilli*, could be demoted to the rank of commoner, or *macehualli*, with loss of all privileges. One of the privileges accorded was eating the meat of sacrificial victims. Although a warrior was forbidden to eat the flesh of his own captives, for each enemy he

captured, he was guaranteed three limbs of a sacrificial victim taken by another warrior. The remaining limb went to the priest classes who conducted the sacrifices, and the skull was hung on the *tzompantli*, the giant skull rack at the base of the pyramid of Huitzilopochtli. The trunk and viscera were given as food to the local zoo animals.

One scholar, Michael Harner of the New School of Social Research in New York, has suggested that the excesses of Aztec sacrifice may not have been solely the result of politics, but may have been a natural reaction to the lack of animal protein available to the ancient Mexicans. There were no domesticated herbivorous sources of meat in the Valley of Mexico, and wild herbivores like deer had been hunted to extinction centuries before the Aztecs arrived. The wholesale eating of human flesh by the nobility may have been a natural, if grotesque, way of adapting.

To cement his military and social system based on sacrificial victims, Tlacaellel apparently rewrote Aztec history to justify the excesses of sacrifice and torture. Tlacaellel and the emperor Itzcoatl organized a deliberate effort to search the temple archives for the glyph books that preserved the earliest Aztec myths and destroy them. The emperor and his general apparently hoped to blot out the memory of deities who were not especially bloodthirsty. Once the old myths were destroyed, they commissioned the court historian, Cuauhcoatl, to write new myths that stressed sacrifice, blood, and carnage.

One unfortunate result of this literary holocaust is that today we really know nothing of the original mythology of the Aztecs except for what we have learned from material that happens to have survived because it was stored in archives outside the reach of the Aztec Empire. For all we know, Aztec mythol-

Replica of a pyramid fresco from Teotihuacan showing corn and the Aztec god Tlaloc.

ogy might once have reflected a much gentler image. For instance, how characteristic of early Aztec mythology is the legend of Xochiquetal, the gentle goddess of flowers, beauty, love, and youth? She protected marriage vows, lovers, the family, and—rather incongruously—prostitutes. Sacrifices to this goddess involved nothing more disturbing than placing bunches of marigolds on her altars.

Of necessity, the Aztec myths that follow are those myths created by Tlacaellel's pet historian-mythographer Cuauhcoatl. Their purpose was to make the history of the Aztecs conform to the brutality of the Aztec state. They are dramatic evidence for the truth of Voltaire's statement that "History is a bag of tricks we play on the dead."

HOW THE AZTECS LEFT THEIR HOMELAND AND SETTLED IN TENOCHTITLAN

In this myth, Cuauhcoatl blended elements that not only explain the origins of the Aztecs, but also show the special relationship they have to the god Huitzilopochtli. This myth also provides "historical" justification for two of the most brutal sacrificial rites of the Aztecs.

This headdress, practically the only surviving example of Aztec feather work, is made of hundreds of quetzal feathers. It is presently in the Museum fuer Voelkerkunde, Vienna, Austria.

helped people preserve their youth. Each level of the mountain represented a different age, with the bottom being equivalent to old age and the top being equivalent to infancy. When people became older than they wanted to be, they merely climbed the mountain until they came to the level corresponding to their desired age; after they rested there awhile, they became younger, until they reached their desired age, and then descended from the mountain.

As the years passed, the other six tribes in Aztlan were drawn by a spirit of adventure to move south to the shores of a great lake between high mountains where there was good farmland and an abundant supply of obsidian. Finally, there was nobody left except the Mexica, who wanted to leave but had no one to lead them.

At about the same time, the goddess Coatlique was sweeping her patio when a brightly colored feather ball came floating down from the sky above. She was interested, but being an industrious goddess, she did not want to stop work. So she stuck out her hand, plucked the ball from the air, and placed it under her blouse, or *huipil*, thinking that she would look at the strange thing later. Coatlique was not a particularly appealing woman— her skirt was made of entwined, living serpents, and around her neck she wore a necklace made of human hearts, severed heads, and hands; her hands and feet ended in sharp claws, and her breasts were wrinkled and hung down to her waist because she had nursed four hundred children fathered by her husband, Mixcoatl, god of the underworld.

When her work was finished, she felt for the ball under the huipil but could not find it. Mystified, she concluded that she had lost it. When she later became pregnant, even though she had not had sex in a very long time, she realized that it was the fault of the feathered ball.

Before the Aztecs lived in the city of Tenochtitlan, on the Great Lake in the Valley of Mexico, they lived far to the north, in a place named Aztlan, the Place of the White Heron. In this early time they were not even called Aztecs, but Mexica, after an early leader named Mecitli.

For years they lived in Aztlan with six other tribes—the Chalca, the Tepanec, the Colhua, the Tlalhuica, the Xochimilca, and the Tlaxcalans—all of which were descended from Iztacmixcohuatl, the mythical founder of the Mexica/Aztecs. Aztlan was a wonderful place with lakes full of fish and fields full of maize. At the center was a high mountain that

After several months, her condition became apparent. Her four hundred children were scandalized, for they knew that their father, Mixcoatl, had been away in his underworld realm for too many months to have had anything to do with her pregnancy.

Her offspring gathered outside her house and threatened to kill her if she did not reveal the name of her lover. Having no name to confess, she remained silent, and the angry children advanced toward her to carry out their threat. Suddenly, the baby she carried, who was the god Huitzilopochtli, burst out of her womb fully formed and slaughtered nearly all of his brothers and sisters. Coatlique did not particularly grieve for her murderous brood, except for her daughter Coyolxauhqui, whose name meant "Golden Bells." Saddened by his mother's grief, Huitzilopochtli cut off Coyolxauhqui's head and threw it high in the sky where it became the moon, so that his mother might take comfort nightly from the sight of her daughter in the sky.

When the people of Aztlan saw Huitzilopochtli carry out the bloody massacre, they realized that here was the man to lead them on their journey to the south.

Huitzilopochtli agreed to lead them, and the band started out. First they came to the land of the fierce Chichimecs, or the Sons of Dogs, who were primitive barbarians who wore no clothing and ate lizards and insects. As was their custom, the Aztecs captured some Chichimecs, then sacrificed and ate them. The Chichimecs tasted so bad, however, that the Aztecs determined from then on to never use them as sacrifices again.

Next the band came to the land of the Michoacans, stopping to rest at a place called Patzcuaro, which was so pleasant that many of the Aztecs wanted to settle there instead of going on the great lake. The leader of those who wished to stay was Malinalxochi, a sister of Huitzilopochtli and one of the few of the four hundred children to survive the massacre. Malinalxochi was beautiful, but she was

A bust of Coyolxauhqui, one of the major goddesses of the Aztecs and the sister of Huitzilopochtli. When their mother, Coatlique, became pregnant, Coyolxauhqui persuaded some of her other brothers to attempt to kill Coatlique. In revenge Huitzilopochtli killed his sister and cut her into pieces. A huge sculpture portraying the severed limbs and torso of Coyolxauhqui has been found at the base of the Templo Mayor in Mexico City.

Jnic. v. parapho ypan mitoa inque
nin mochichivaya yrerryaca teteu.

paynal.

vitzilopuchtli.

(1)

(2)

(3)

tezcatlipuca.

quezalcoatl.

chicomecoatl

chachalmeca

(4)

(7)

(10)

totochtin.

otontecuhtli

yxcocauhqui

(5)

(8)

(11)

tlalloc.

yacatecutli

ixtlilto.

(6)

(9)

(12)

also a deadly sorceress whose special talent was commanding the scorpions, snakes, and other stinging, biting creatures of the desert. Aware of her power, Huitzilopochtli chose not to oppose her openly, but pretended to agree with her decision to stay. He suggested that Malinalxochi and her followers take a bath in a nearby river to prepare for a sacrifice that would sanctify their new home in Patzcuaro. When they were all in the river, Huitzilopochtli and those loyal to him stole all of their clothes and sandals so that the bathers could not follow through the harsh desert climate. Malinalxochi cursed her brother and swore that she would get revenge.

For many years, the Aztecs continued to migrate slowly to the south. Sometimes they stopped for a year to plant crops or fight their way through a group of people who resented their presence. Finally, after twenty years, the band of emigrants came to Tula, located about sixty miles (96km) north of the Valley of Mexico. Here Huitzilopochtli ordered the Aztecs to build a dam to make a lake around which they could settle for a time—he wanted them fresh and strong for the fight he knew faced them in the valley. But the lake was too pleasant, and a large number of people wanted to stay. Again, Huitzilopochtli pretended to agree, but later that same night he gathered together his most faithful followers and wandered with them through the sleeping Aztecs, picking out those who had been most vocal in demanding to stay at Tula, and slicing open their chests to tear out their hearts. When the remaining Aztecs awoke the next morning, they saw the ground littered with mutilated corpses. When Huitzilopochtli told them that he was responsible, they all agreed that they did not want to settle in Tula.

Unfortunately for the Aztecs, they were expected but not welcomed. The evil Malinalxochi, still thirsting for revenge, had sent her son, Copil, to stir up the people of the valley

against the Aztecs. Copil told the people that the Aztecs were evil, dirty, and not to be trusted. With advance publicity like that, it was no surprise that everybody attacked the Aztecs. The most fierce attacks came from the Tepanecs of the city of Azcapotzalco. The Tepanecs defeated the Aztecs and drove them south into the territory of the Culhuaque, though not before Huitzilopochtli killed Copil, ripped out his heart, and flung it far out into the lake.

The Culhuaque did not especially want the Aztecs in their territory, and for a time their king, Coxcoxtli, thought about killing them all. But then he thought of an easier way to be rid of these rude barbarians. He allowed them to settle in some swampy land south of Colhuacan called Tizipan. The Culhuaque had always avoided this place because it swarmed with huge rattlesnakes. The snakes might have defeated lesser tribes, but Huitzilopochtli told his people that the snakes were good to eat, and they devoured all of the disagreeable reptiles.

A modern painting of the floating garden plots called *chinampas*, which could support two crop plantings each year and were kept in place by willow trees planted along the edges. Thousands of these chinampas surrounded Tenochtitlan on every side.

Next, the Aztecs built a temple pyramid to honor Huitzilopochtli, and then began to plant crops. When Coxcoxtli heard about the snakes, the pyramid, and the crops, he went to visit, bringing his large army. The Aztecs showed him their crops and even took him to the top of their pyramid, where they had erected an altar. But Coxcoxtli insulted the Aztecs. He said their crops were poor and then defecated on the altar of Huitzilopochtli. The Aztecs held their tempers because they were not strong enough to fight the huge army; Huitzilopochtli, however, told them there would soon be a time for revenge.

Soon after, Coxcoxtli goaded the Aztecs to attack the city of Xochimilco by telling the Aztecs that the city was rich and had a weak army. In fact, they had a strong army, and Coxcoxtli was hoping that the Xochimilque

would destroy the Aztecs. Of course, it did not turn out that way, for the Aztecs beat the Xochimilque and dragged home thousands of prisoners to sacrifice to Huitzilopochtli. The prisoners were sacrificed on the holy hearth, a bed of red-hot coals on which prisoners were first roasted and then dragged out, still living, to have their hearts torn out. When Coxcoxtli came to witness the horrible sacrifices at the invitation of the Aztecs, the king was so impressed that he decided these people might be more useful as allies than as enemies, and he determined to make peace with them. He even gave the Aztec king, Acamapichtli, one of his daughters to marry.

Unfortunately, Huitzilopochtli was not ready to make peace—he still smarted under the insult of King Coxcoxtli's defecation on top of his temple. The revenge planned by the

Aztec god was terrible, even by Aztec standards. He ordered the poor daughter of Coxcoxtli killed and skinned, then dressed one of the Aztec warriors in the skin of the murdered girl and invited the king to come to visit. When Coxcoxtli first entered the audience hall, he thought he saw King Acamapichtli and his daughter seated at the far end, but because the interior was dark he could not see that his "daughter" was really a man wearing the girl's skin. Only when he got closer did he realize the terrible truth and run screaming from the room. He didn't hesitate to return to Colhuacan, collect his army, and return to punish these horrible people. But he was too late—the Aztecs, anticipating this vengeance, had already departed for two low swampy islands in the lake, where they were well hidden from the king's vengeance.

Huitzilopochtli had learned in a vision that he was to take the Aztecs to these islands. According to the vision, one of these islands was the same island where he had thrown the heart of Copil, the son of Malinalxochi. This heart, so the legend claimed, had landed in a swamp and grown into a prickly pear cactus. Now Huitzilopochtli was to search the islands for that cactus plant. He would know the right plant when he saw it—perched on the cactus would be an eagle holding a white snake in its talons. On that exact spot, the Aztecs were to raise a great pyramid, around which they would build a city. The city was to be called Tenochtitlan, the Place of the Prickly Pear Cactus.

Unfortunately, the island where Huitzilopochtli found the cactus and the bird belonged to the fierce Tepaneca from Azcapotzalco, whose king sent word to the Aztecs that they had to leave the islands. Huitzilopochtli responded by offering to do any task the king ordered; if he succeeded, the island would belong to the Aztecs, but if he failed, the Aztecs would become Tepanec slaves forever. The king asked Huitzilopochtli to grow crops on the water of the lake, a seemingly impossible task. Huitzilopochtli was equal to the challenge, however. To accomplish this task, he invented the chinampas, the huge baskets that were filled with rich earth and anchored to the lake bottom. The Tepanec king, having given his word, had no choice but to let the Aztecs stay.

THE MYTH OF THE FIFTH SUN

The Aztecs lived in a world where they expected the worst. Not only were they surrounded by human enemies on all sides, but nature also conspired against them. They firmly believed, for instance, that the sun might disappear, leaving them in utter darkness. The most important ceremony of their busy religious calendar occurred every fifty-two years, when their two calendar systems—one of 260 days, the other of 365 days—came into alignment: the beginning of each year fell on the same day. At this time, they truly believed that the sun might go out unless the Sun God, Huitzilopochtli, was placated with

Symbols for four days of the Aztec month. The days are named Jaguar, Eagle, Vulture, and Earthquake. There were twenty distinct days and these were paired with the numbers 1 through 13 (dots above the figures) to make 260 days of the religious calendar. Reading from the right, therefore, we have 4 Jaguar, 5 Eagle, 6 Vulture, and 7 Earthquake.

Maize stored in a tree
near present-day
Mexico City to keep
it from mice.

thousands of human sacrifices and many days of complicated ritual. Between the fifty-two-year events, the Sun God needed to be appeased with an annual sacrifice of one thousand hearts at every sun temple throughout the empire.

According to their myths, the sun had gone out four times before, necessitating the creation of a new sun and earth, as well as new humans, each time. The cause of this terrible calamity had always been the impiety of mankind. The first time, the people refused to worship the gods correctly, and the deities had sent jaguars to devour all of the impious wretches. The second time, the people had also sinned and not worshiped appropriately, and the gods, for punishment, had turned them into monkeys. The third time, lack of

adequate sacrifice had forced the gods to destroy the whole world by fire—nothing survived except the birds who could fly high above the flames. The fourth time, the gods had destroyed the world with a great flood. Again mankind had perished, except for two people, a man and wife whose pitiful cries had persuaded the gods to spare them. The gods instructed the couple to climb into a huge tree with a supply of maize and ride out the flood as it swirled around the tree. They were instructed to eat only the maize and nothing else. But, unfortunately, when the waters receded, the couple saw the ground littered with dead fish and decided to cook some. They kindled a fire and began to fry some, but the gods smelled the fish cooking and turned the husband and wife into dogs as punishment.

After this the gods decided to live without people—they were tired of these ungrateful creatures. But they soon grew tired of having no one to worship them and decided to try again. But for this the gods needed a new sun.

Now the only way to create a sun is for a god to burn himself up in a huge fire so that his burning body ignites the cold, dead sun. So the gods gathered together to determine which of them would volunteer to climb into a fire and destroy himself for the good of all. Most of them were surprised when Nanautzin, the god of disease, volunteered. He was the least popular of all the gods because he was so ugly—he was covered with sores, he suffered from leprosy, and he had a hump on his back. Perhaps his physical appearance made the other gods distrust him; many of them said that such an ugly fellow would not have the courage to jump into the fire when the time came.

"He's just putting on a show to gain a little credit. He'll never go through with it," said Tezcatlipoca, the god of war, who was naturally distrustful. "We ought to choose another just in case—someone we can depend on."

The rest of the gods agreed. Teciciztecatl, the god of wealth, stepped forward. He was beautifully dressed, famed for his extravagance, and very popular. Everybody agreed that he was a much better choice than Nanautzin.

On the appointed day, after a great fire had been prepared and fed for four days, Teciciztecatl stepped forward and crouched as if to jump into the fire. But at the last moment he stepped back, for the thought of burning to death, despite the fame it would bring him, was too much for him. There was a collective groan from the assembled gods, and this moved Teciciztecatl to try once more. But again he lost his nerve and stepped back. Twice more he tried, but in the end, he simply hung his head and walked away. It seemed there would be no new sun, no new world, and no people to worship the gods and feed their pride.

But everybody had forgotten Nanautzin. The ugly, misshapen creature stepped forward and, with only a moment's hesitation, threw himself headlong into the fire. His clothing and hair caught fire, and the flames shot into the air, igniting the cold, dead ball of the sun.

Stone of the Sun. An Aztec calendar stone for the 365-day calendar. The Aztecs had two calendars, one of 260 days with thirteen months of twenty days each, and another of 365 days with eighteen months of twenty days each plus five unlucky days at the end.

The gods cheered and praised Nanautzin. Tecicíztecatl, shamed by the action of Nanautzin, finally gathered the courage to step forward, and he, too, stepped into the fire and was consumed. The earth was bathed in light and warmth, and all the gods learned a lesson—that it is unwise to judge anyone by his appearance. Some say that Nanautzin's soul, when it finished its four-year journey through Mictlan, the land of the dead, was reborn in the body of the great Quetzalcoatl, the most handsome and best loved of all the gods.

QUETZALCOATL: THE GREAT BENEFACTOR OF MANKIND

The most famous god of the Aztec pantheon was Quetzalcoatl, whose worship did not originate with the Aztecs, but in fact extends far back into Mesoamerican history. The Toltecs worshiped this powerful diety in their capital

The main stairway to the top of the pyramid of Quetzalcoatl at Teotihuacan. The heads are those of the feathered serpent Quetzalcoatl.

of Tula during the tenth century A.D. At the city of Teotihuacan, which flourished between A.D. 1 and 600, there are stone heads carved on the edges of the staircases that appear to be images of the god.

The popularity of this god undoubtedly had to do with the legends of his benefits to humankind. Not only did he create the physical features of the world, but he also created humankind and gave them maize. There is evidence that the earliest worship of Quetzalcoatl was unique in that it did not require human sacrifice, but by the time of the Aztecs worship of the god required the annual slaughter of thousands of human beings, a fact in which the bloody hand of Tlacaellel and his reworking of ancient myths were no doubt present.

The ancient legends say that after the creation of the fifth sun the gods noted that the world was without form. There was a sun in the sky, but the only feature on the planet's surface was an unending sea in which a huge, monstrous, vaguely female creature swam. This monster was so large that when she splashed on one side of the world, tidal waves appeared on the other side. Her appetite was so tremendous that there was a danger that she would eat all of the fish in the sea. Furthermore, wherever land broke the surface of the vast worldwide sea, the splashing and thrashing of this leviathan washed it away.

Looking down from the heavens, Quetzalcoatl realized the danger presented by this huge creature and decided to do something about it. He asked his friend Tezcatlipoca to help him and the two dived into the sea and attacked this monster. While Texcatlipocha distracted the monster, Quetzalcoatl swung his great obsidian sword and cut the creature's belly open, spilling her internal organs into the sea.

Then Tezcatlipoca and Quetzalcoatl cut the huge corpse into pieces. They formed the

continents out of her viscera and body parts and created grass, flowers, and other growing things from her hair. They made deep lakes from her eyes; rivers from her saliva; caves from her mouth, ears, and nostrils; and mountains from her nose and breasts. Her tears became the rain.

Understandably, the goddess was unhappy, and her severed body parts often shook with anger, causing earthquakes. The only way to please her was to periodically sacrifice human blood to her. So while the goddess's death made life possible for humankind, those same humans found that they in turn also had to make sacrifices.

Quetzalcoatl represented as coming out of the earth, which is depicted as the mouth of a wolf. This head, which was found at Tula, is made of shell.

los q̃ nacion a qⁱy ꞇᵘᵉ̃
en ᵭ hombreſ Ricos

But that was later—when the goddess was cut up into pieces to form the features of the world, human beings did not yet exist. It was necessary to create them, and the gods assembled together in council to decide how best to accomplish this. Again it was the wise Quetzalcoatl who provided the solution. He decided to travel to the underworld, which was called Mictlan, and ask Mictlantecuhtli, the god of that realm, for the return of the bones of his father, the god Xochipilli. Once he had these bones, he would grind them into powder, draw blood from his tongue and penis, and sprinkle the blood over the powder to make a paste from which he would fashion humans.

At first Mictlantecuhtli did not want to give Quetzalcoatl the bones, but Quetzalcoatl promised that mankind would be grateful and sacrifice many hearts and much blood to Mictlantecuhtli. Like all the gods, Mictlantecuhtli was greedy for glory and worship, and so he gave Quetzalcoatl the bones and Quetzalcoatl crafted men and women to populate the earth.

Soon after the creation of humankind, another problem presented itself. Human beings proved to be so prolific that they soon outstripped their food supply—at this time people ate only fruits from the trees and hunted for meat. To find meat they had to wander the earth, which meant they did not have time to worship the gods or to build great temples and pyramids in their honor. Because of this the gods felt cheated—humankind was not spending enough time in worship—and some even talked among themselves about destroying humankind altogether. Quetzalcoatl, disturbed by this, tried to think of a solution—there had to be some way for human beings to find enough to eat and still have time to worship the gods.

One day he saw a tiny ant carrying a yellow kernel of maize out from under a rock. The god, who was always curious, took the kernel from the ant and tasted it. It was delicious, and Quetzalcoatl realized that he had found the ideal food source for humankind. If people could grow this delicious food, they could settle in one place and have time to build temples and pyramids and to worship the gods.

Quetzalcoatl quickly changed himself into an ant and joined the procession of ants bringing out maize from under the rock. All day, Quetzalcoatl labored with his insect brothers. Finally, at the end of the day, he had collected a huge bag of maize. He planted the kernels, and when they were grown, brought the leaders of men together to show them the wonderful food. All agreed that it was much better to grow maize than to hunt through the world for animals.

Quetzalcoatl's discovery made life better for both human beings and the gods, and everyone—human and divine—rejoiced, saying that Quetzalcoatl was the greatest god.

But as often happens, this popularity bred jealousy. Tezcatlipoca, the god of war, feeling that Quetzalcoatl was too popular, decided to get rid of him. The war god asked Tlazolteotl, the goddess of drunkenness and lust, to help him. She brewed a special wine that was so good that no one could resist it. Tezcatlipoca tempted Quetzalcoatl with the wine. At first, Quetzalcoatl refused to drink it, but when Tezcatlipoca insisted, he took a sip. His eyes lit up, and he took another drink and then another. He drained the cup and demanded more. He drank cup after cup until he was terribly drunk. Once Quetzalcoatl was reeling with drunkenness, Tlazolteotl dressed in her most beautiful garments, put on perfume, and painted her face to enhance her beauty. She easily seduced the befuddled god. They spent the night together, and just before dawn the wicked goddess changed herself into the image of Quet-

This large jaguar effigy (87 x 47 x 37 inches [221 x 120 x 94cm]) made from volcanic stone, which was found at the Templo Mayor in Mexico City, contains a depression called a quauhxicalli, or "eagle's nest," to hold a vivisected human heart. The inside of the quauhxicalli is decorated with stylized eagle feathers.

In this depiction of
Quetzalcoatl from the
Florentine Codex,
the god wears quetzal
feathers on his head
and back.

zalcoatl's own sister, Xochiquetal, the goddess of flowers, the family, and marriage vows. Meanwhile, Tezcatlipoca had summoned all the other gods to the house of Quetzalcoatl.

When the gods entered, it appeared that Quetzalcoatl had seduced his own sister, for she was lying next to him in bed. When the god awoke, he was also convinced that he had done this horrible thing. Shamed beyond bearing, Quetzalcoatl decided to leave forever. He built a raft of serpents and sailed away into the east.

It did not take long for the gods to discover the cruel trick, but by then it was too late, for they could not find Quetzalcoatl. Without the help of the benevolent god, the work of mankind became infinitely harder. Without him, Tezcatlipoca reigned supreme, and war became continuous.

Still the people hoped for Quetzalcoatl's return, and a legend grew that Quetzalcoatl would someday return to help the Aztecs once again. Many believed that Quetzalcoatl, just before he sailed away, had said he would return on Ce-Acatl, a date in the Aztec calendar that was equivalent to the Christian year 1363, 1467, or 1519.

It was a fortunate coincidence for Hernando Cortés and his army that they landed on the east coast of Mexico in 1519. For the Aztecs, the powerful weapons, ships, armor, and horses of this army certainly qualified as the kind of supernatural things that might accompany the return of a powerful god like Quetzalcoatl. For a short time at least, the hope that Cortés might actually be Quetzalcoatl caused the Aztecs to delay dealing forcefully with the Spanish invader. This delay provided enough time for Cortés to establish a foothold on the coast and establish alliances with the Indian enemies of the Aztecs. It is one of the supreme ironies of history that the legend predicting the return of Quetzalcoatl to help the Aztec people would turn out to be the leading cause of their being conquered and destroyed.

The surrender of Cuauhtemoc to Cortés. When Montezuma died of smallpox, Cuauhtemoc, his son-in-law, took command of the Aztec army. He conducted a spirited defense of the capital Tenochtitlan. Had he been in command from the first contact with the Spanish, he might have beaten Cortés because he recommended attacking the Spaniards in the narrow mountain passes before they reached the Valley of Mexico.

THE INCA WORLD

At the same time that the emperor Itzcoatl and his nephew, the psychopathic commander-in-chief Tlacaellel, were transforming the Valley of Mexico into a unified "nation" under Aztec rule, a much more humane leader was unifying the Indian population of northwestern South America into an empire that dwarfed the Aztec state. The great Inca leader Pachacuti (1415?–1471) was one of those personalities who seems to transform the history of his country all by himself.

A romanticized painting of the Inca king Pachacuti, his wife, and his favorite dwarf. Like the ancient Egyptian rulers, the Inca kings were fascinated by dwarfs.

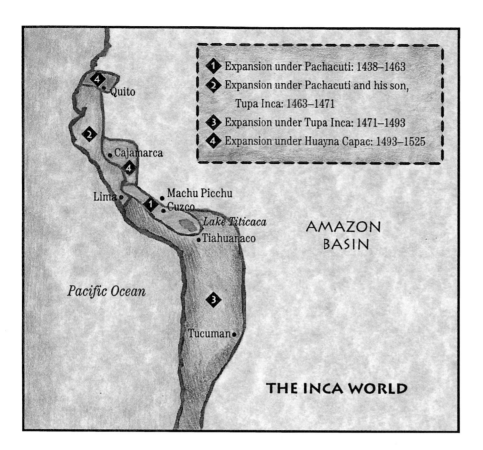

The map legend reads:

1. Expansion under Pachacuti: 1438–1463
2. Expansion under Pachacuti and his son, Tupa Inca: 1463–1471
3. Expansion under Tupa Inca: 1471–1493
4. Expansion under Huayna Capac: 1493–1525

Quito

Cajamarca

Lima · Machu Picchu · Cuzco

Lake Titicaca · Tiahuanaco

AMAZON BASIN

Pacific Ocean

Tucuman·

THE INCA WORLD

RIGHT: An Inca model of a mummy bundle. The important nobles of the Incas felt it was mandatory to be mummified at death. The dry climate, not special embalming techniques, were the secret to the bodies' survival.

Without Pachacuti, the people we call the Incas (although properly only the ruler was called Inca—everybody else was just a subject) would have been just one of two dozen tribes that inhabited the area around the valley of the Huatanay River in what is today Peru. Because of Pachacuti, however, the Incas became conquerors and came to dominate an empire stretching twenty-six hundred miles (4,160km), from Ecuador to southern Chile.

The Incas' rise to power certainly began inauspiciously enough. In A.D. 1438 a tribe called the Chancas attacked Cuzco, the capital of the Incas. The Inca king, Viracocha, had for several years been making a pest of himself by attacking the surrounding tribes and claiming to be the descendant of Viracocha, the Sun God. The Chancas, who themselves claimed descent from the godlike mountain lion, decided to end the pretensions of this upstart. They gathered a large army and advanced toward Cuzco. When Viracocha learned the size of the army moving against him, he forgot his claims of greatness, packed

his harem and his eldest son, Urcon, off to the mountains, and abandoned Cuzco to the enemy. At that moment, the Incas could have become just another historical footnote. But Pachacuti, Viracocha's youngest son, was not cut out to be a footnote. He organized an army, and to the surprise of the Chancas, he refused to be shut up in the city for a siege. He boldly attacked, drove straight through the Chanca lines, captured the image of their mountain lion god, and sent them running back to the hills. After the battle, at a loss to explain a victory that only luck could account for, Pachacuti claimed that the very rocks of the valley had magically changed into Inca soldiers and aided his attack. Ever after, when the Incas went into battle they carried with them litters filled with stones named for departed warriors, just in case there was a need for reinforcements.

After the victory, Pachacuti celebrated accordingly, by drinking chicha—a brew made of maize kernels that are chewed up and spit

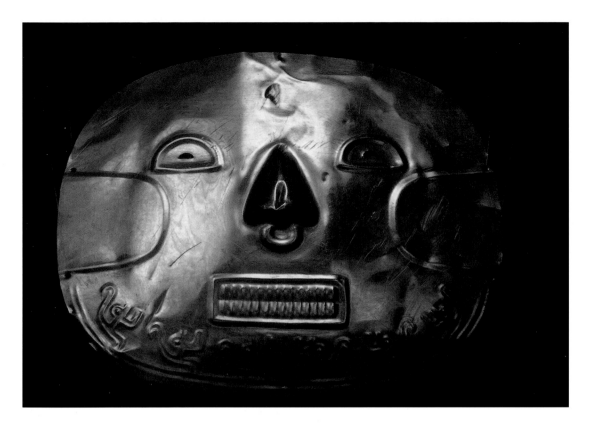

into a bowl to ferment—out of a Chanca skull, and then sat back to think about how the Inca nation could be improved. In the end, he de- termined to remake the country from the top down, and in the next few years he did just that. He completely reorganized the govern- ment, the social structure, the economy, and the religion of his people. In so doing he cre- ated the most authoritarian, absolute rule of any nation at any time in history.

But first there was the problem of his fa- ther and elder brother—Pachacuti had no use for incompetents, no matter what their con- nections. It is not clear what happened to these relatives—they just disappeared. The nobles of Cuzco elected Pachacuti emperor, and he launched his reform program. He con- tinued his father's claim that he was the Sun God, Viracocha, and he backed it up with an impressive rebuilding campaign. Under his rule, Cuzco became a *huaca*, a holy place. There were huacas all over the Andes, but Pachacuti made Cuzco *the* huaca. He tore down the old city and rebuilt it completely. Whereas before it had been a city of adobe

and thatch, now it was a city of stone. The Huatanay River was channeled and made to flow underneath the city. At the southern end of Cuzco, he built the Coricancha, the Sun Temple, to celebrate the Sun God—himself. The Sun Temple was huge; according to one Spanish witness, it was twelve hundred feet (365.8m) in circumference. Inside were chap- els to the moon, the planet Venus, thunder, lightning, and the rainbow. The temple also held the mummies of earlier Inca rulers, each of whom had his own attendants and altar.

The temple walls were covered with gold—unbelievable amounts of gold. Pedro Sancho, a Spaniard, reported that the walls were covered with hundreds of golden plates, each of which weighed four and a half pounds (2kg). In his reports, he states that the Span- ish stripped the walls and carried off two hun- dred loads of these golden plates to be melted into bullion. One such load, he claims, con- tained seven hundred plates. A quick calcula- tion will reveal that the Spaniard was talking about 3,150 pounds (1,430.1kg) of gold in a single load, which means that the Spanish stole 630,000 pounds (286,020kg) of gold from the Incas (which at today's price of $380 dollars an ounce [28g], would be worth about $3.8 billion).

Such numbers would sound made up if they were not matched by other gargantuan statistics that grew out of the projects Pachacuti completed before the Spanish arrived. At the northern end of "New Cuzco," Pachacuti built Sacsahuaman, a great fortress that was supposed to protect Cuzco. Three sides of this mighty fortress are protected by sheer cliffs. The northern side is protected by three parallel walls, each of which is four hundred feet (121.9m) long and sixty feet (18.3m) high. These walls are built of thousands of stones weighing one hundred tons (90.7t) each, yet the stones are fitted so exactly that it is difficult to insert a knife blade between two stones—a fact that thousands of modern-day tourists test each year. To further take one's

Sacsahuaman, the huge fortress outside Cuzco, was ninety years in the building and was still not finished when the Inca Empire fell to the Spanish. The design of this fortress included three parallel walls built in a zigzag pattern so that attackers assaulting one wall would always be forced to present their sides and backs to defenders on another wall.

breath away, the majority of the hundred-ton stones came from a quarry twelve miles (19.2km) away. Garcilaso de La Vega, the half-Inca, half-Spanish chronicler of ancient Peru, claims that twenty thousand workers were needed to move each stone from the quarry to Sacsahuaman.

Pachacuti did not stop with these two buildings, however. He built the Aclla-huaci, the school and dormitory for the four thousand virgins who became members of his harem, served as wives for favored nobles, acted as priestesses for various temples, or were used as sacrificial victims. Like their northern neighbors, the Maya and Aztecs, the Incas practiced human sacrifice—although they never killed as many people. Human sacrifice was reserved for the most important occasions or the darkest catastrophe. The crowning of a new emperor, Pachacuti decreed, would involve the sacrifice of two hun-

dred perfectly formed and unblemished children. Famine, disease, or military defeat also necessitated a sacrifice. And after a successful military conquest, prisoners of war were brought to Cuzco and sacrificed.

Besides the Aclla-huaci, Pachacuti's building and landscaping program produced temples and extensive gardens all over the city. There were more than a hundred temples throughout Cuzco and dozens of gardens full of trees and flowers. He also built temples and fortresses throughout the empire. All this required massive numbers of men who had to be fed, clothed, and directed in their tasks. The success of his programs is a monument to the tightly regimented structure of Inca society as organized by Pachacuti.

Geographically speaking, the Inca Empire was not a hospitable place. Its western border

was the Pacific coast, noted as the most extreme desert environment in the world—there are large portions of this desert in which not a drop of rain has fallen in the nearly five hundred years since Europeans started keeping records. To the east of this desert are the great Andean Mountains, the highest in the western hemisphere. The steep mountain slopes make farming difficult—a difficulty the Incas overcame by building thousands of terraces into the mountain sides and then filling them with soil carried from the few scattered, fertile valleys. Behind the Andes is the beginning of the great Amazon jungle with its heat and humidity and fierce tribes that the Incas were never able to conquer.

It is to the credit of Pachacuti and his son Tupa Inca that they molded this diverse area, which was home to more than a hundred dif-

A border post guarding the eastern frontier of the Incas against the Amazon Indians. The Inca armies were never able to penetrate very far into the Amazon jungle—this was partially because of the climate and partially because of the fierce inhabitants.

ferent tribes, into a tight political entity that could feed and clothe millions of people, support massive building programs, and supply huge armies operating a thousand miles (1,600km) from their base.

The biggest task was producing enough maize and potatoes in this inhospitable environment to feed the citizens of the empire, and enough cotton to clothe everybody. The great problem was that no single area in the Empire produced all three—maize, potatoes, and cotton needed to be collected from different areas and distributed throughout the realm. Maize grew on the lower western slopes of the Andes up to sixty-five hundred feet (1,981.2m). Potatoes grew above this height up to fourteen thousand feet (4,267.2m). And cotton grew on the eastern jungle slope of the Andes. Throughout the empire, each village produced what its ecosystem dictated, consumed exactly what it needed, and sent the rest away to support other villages, receiving

in turn items they could not grow themselves. Produce was not sold or bartered—it was shared in a very real version of Karl Marx's injunction, "each according to ability, each according to need." Any surplus was stored in warehouses until it was needed to support armies or work crews building roads, temples, or official buildings. The system worked because everyone was "frozen" into a specific task and social position, and these parameters were enforced according to strict laws governing laziness and preventing variant behavior. Nobody could leave their village except for periodic stints in the army or to serve as a member of an official work crew.

Throughout the Inca Empire, every man, woman, and child was assigned a specific task, and each person performed his or her task in a kind of trance, day after day, month after month. Children over five were expected to carry water to workers in the fields, women over fifty were delegated to weave, and men

Peruvian Indians known as the Quechua, ancestors of the ancient Inca, overlooking typical farmland around Cuzco. It was on land like this that the Inca grew their maize. The land to the west, which was lower in elevation, was where the Inca grew their cotton, and the land above this altitude was where the Inca grew most of their potatoes.

LEFT: A reenactment of the Inti-raymi festival, in which corn and potatoes are offered to the god of the sun. In some Inca accounts, Inti was the Sun god and the father of Viracocha, the god responsible for teaching mankind how to be civilized.

BELOW: Quipu strings from the archaeological collection in Lima. Different colors combined with different knots helped the memory. Scholars believe that these strings were used to keep tallies of goods or to record work done by various citizens.

over fifty were employed to walk about the fields scaring birds away from the crops. Even mentally defective and physically disabled people were given tasks commensurate with their abilities—they fulfilled their duty to the empire by sitting all day, chewing maize and spitting it into bowls to start the fermentation process that produced chicha—the alcoholic beverage of the Incas. Each person's duty was carefully recorded by officials who kept such records on various colored strings tied with different types of knots called *quipus*. The conquering Spaniards marveled at the accuracy of this system.

Coercion seems to have played a very small role in the system. Most people did what they did willingly, in part because Pachacuti allowed for periodic breaks. He knew that "all work and no play" made a dull Inca, and so, six times a month, the empire "stopped." Everyone walked to the nearest town or village, watched pageants, heard speeches, and chewed coca leaves. The coca leaf, which today's drug lords use to produce cocaine, gave people a mild buzz when they chewed it. The Inca nobility were allowed to

chew the leaf whenever they pleased, but the peasants could do so only on the special festival days. And the peasants were so well disciplined that they actually followed this rule.

In addition to holidays and coca leaves, Pachacuti used religion to inspire his people to work for the good of the empire. Early in his reign he completely reorganized the Inca religion. First, he moved to destroy the power of the priest class and assume that power for himself. Before Pachacuti had come into

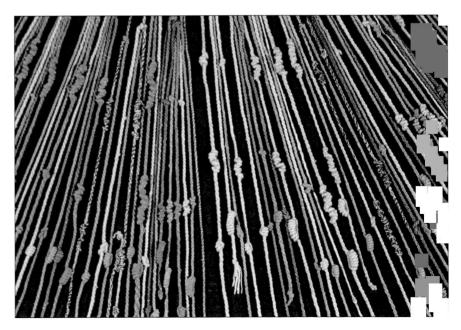

power, each local priest had enjoyed dictatorial power over a specific, small area. Many of these priests had even assumed a quasidivine character to awe the common people. Pachacuti usurped this divine nature—and the powers that came with it—for himself. He took his father's claim to be Viracocha—the Sun god. By doing so, Pachacuti convinced his subjects that to do their assigned tasks was to worship Viracocha, who in turn would see to their well-being, health, and entertainment.

To emphasize his godlike nature, Pachacuti created a special mystique for Viracocha. As Viracocha, Pachacuti and all the emperors who succeeded him lived in the greatest luxury: they wore new clothes every day (the previous day's were burned), ate only from golden plates and bowls, and traveled in a litter carried by the highest nobles of the state. His spit was considered too sacred to fall on the ground, so he expectorated into the palm of a handmaiden who then swallowed the sacred moisture. Any hair that fell from his head was carefully gathered up and eaten by a servant. His sacred character also meant that he

could not marry just anyone—only his sister was sacred enough to be his wife, although he condescended to share his bed with any one of three hundred lesser consorts. (Later emperors, such as Atahualpa, had as many as four thousand concubines.)

Pachacuti also created a noble lineage for himself. He carefully collected what he claimed were the mummies of his nine predecessors and housed them in the great temple of Coricancha, where they were served by their own staff of virgins who ceremoniously fed them, flicked the flies away, and clothed their withered limbs in beautiful textiles. Periodically, the mummies were taken from the temple and displayed to the people in elaborate ceremonies.

It was at these ceremonies that Pachacuti sought to impress his subjects with the magnificence of the god Viracocha—himself—and the importance of their fulfilling their individual duties to keep the empire strong and therefore ensure that they themselves were protected all from harm. One especially impressive ceremony was the Situa, which protected the people from disease. This rite took place in August, at the beginning of the rainy season, whose dampness usually brought plagues and disease. At the start of this three-day ceremony, the mummies of the Emperor's ancestors were brought out, and holy objects that had been brought from all over the empire were assembled in the Great Plaza at the center of Cuzco. Dogs, people with deformities, and those whose earlobes had broken were driven out of the town. (One of the customs of the Incas involved the insertion of disks of various types in their earlobes. This began in childhood, when they pierced their lobes and inserted small disks; over time, these disks were replaced with gradually larger disks, until some were three of four inches [7.6–10.2cm] in diameter. Of course, this stretched the skin to such an extent that it

sometimes broke. A broken earlobe was interpreted as divine punishment, and those who suffered this wound were forbidden to be present at religious ceremonies.)

Once the unclean elements had been driven from Cuzco, the rest of the population gathered in the Great Plaza, where four hundred of the bravest soldiers had assembled. A group of one hundred soldiers faced each of the four cardinal compass points and shouted in unison for all disease, illness, and disasters to leave the empire. The cry was taken up by the spectators, who then went to the Huatanay River to bathe and wash away all their sins and diseases. Next everyone lit a straw torch and marched through the city to their homes, where they smeared their faces with a specially prepared paste of maize and water called *sancu*. Any family of nobles that had

A modern-day recreation of the sun ceremony performed at the base of Sacsahuaman.

Skilled gold work on a copper base. Beautiful gold work was not unique to the Incas. The Chimu of the north coast made this humorous representation of a cat's face from gold. The Chimu, who had their capital at Chan-Chan, were the first people to make three-dimensional gold ornaments by hammering the precious metal around a wooden mold. The Chimu are credited with teaching the Inca how to work gold.

mummies also smeared the corpse with this paste. Afterward, everybody settled down to a feast in the Great Plaza where nobles encouraged everyone to eat as much as they liked.

The next day in the Plaza a huge golden image of a man representing Viracocha, the Sun god, and a great golden circle representing the orb of the sun was smeared with sancu. Other images, also made of gold, were displayed, and the rest of the day was also spent eating and drinking.

Finally, on the third day of the ceremony, thousands of llamas were driven into the Great Plaza and the priests selected four of the most perfect animals for sacrifice. Priests mixed the blood of these animals with a sacred maize meal that was then distributed to the assembly. Each person ate a small morsel of the mixture after promising never to say anything bad about the sun or ever to be unfaithful to the emperor.

The innovations begun by Pachacuti were continued by his son Tupa Inca. The religious innovations made possible an empirewide organization that allowed for a rapid expansion

to the north and south. Inca armies pushed the empire's frontiers 150 miles (240km) north of modern Quito, Ecuador, and 150 miles (240km) south of Santiago, Chile. Only to the east, where the Incas met the green hell of the Amazon jungle and its fierce tribes, did the expansion stop.

The system of Pachacuti worked well as long as there was a strong ruler. When Tupa died in 1493, he was succeeded by Huayna Capac (reigned 1493–1525), an able ruler and administrator who unfortunately insisted on breaking tradition by refusing to take his own sister as his principal wife and taking instead a Quito princess. All the holy men and soothsayers of Cuzco warned that the empire would suffer terrible consequences as a result of Huayna Capac's breaking of his incestuous marriage vows to his sister. This brother-sister marriage had already produced a son named Huascar, but his marriage to the Quito temptress produced another son, Atahualpa. Both men claimed the throne when their father died. With two claimants for the throne, the empire broke into civil war. The timing of this was especially unfortunate, for as war raged Francisco Pizarro and his Spanish followers invaded the empire and destroyed it in the most vicious and barbaric attack ever undertaken by Europeans on any Indian society. Had Inca society been united under a capable ruler, the Spaniards, faced with the formidable terrain of Peru, might not have been so fortunate.

Although the Incas as a society were destroyed by Pizarro, their myths live on—the legacy of Pachacuti includes not only his glorious buildings but also the bloody myths that he, like the Aztec ruler Itzcoatl, created for his own political needs. Pachacuti sought to solidify his rule by inventing some legends and recasting other traditional elements of Inca society to support his fundamental restructuring of the culture as well as his claim to divine descent from the Sun god. Perhaps even the mummies that Pachacuti claimed were the remains of his divine ancestors were just some

obscure corpses taken from an old burial and presented as relatives, after Pachacuti had invented great deeds for them. Most modern scholars believe that the activities of all seven Inca rulers before Pachacuti's father, Viracocha, were almost completely Pachacuti's invention. Pachacuti's mythological creations appear to be an attempt to emphasize his own special status and thereby ensure his political power through identification with gods that predate his rise to power. His myths were also a tool to prove to the non-Inca people he conquered that all culture, technology, and learning originated from Inca gods, therefore establishing the racial superiority of the Incas.

Although it may sound farfetched to suppose that people would so easily accept Pachacuti's fables and quickly forget their own mythology, we must remember that the Incas were preliterate—they had no other means than oral history by which to preserve the

The Uruhamba River Valley. This valley east of Cuzco was one of the first areas conquered by Pachacuti. The famous city Machu Picchu is built high above this river. The last emperor of the Incas, Manco Capac, retreated to this relatively isolated valley and defied the Spanish for thirty years.

RIGHT: At 12,506 feet (3,812m), Lake Titicaco, which straddles the Bolivian-Peruvian border, is the highest in the world. It is found in a basin between the Cordillera Oriental and the Andes Mountains. There are Inca ruins on two islands in the southern end of the lake. According to legend, Viracocha and his wife, Mamacocha, lived in the lake prior to coming forth to found the Inca race.

BELOW: An Inca rendition of a maize plant made out of solid silver. Maize was used to make *chicha*, the Incan beer.

memory of their own past. If a ruler like Pachacuti was able to control not only the military and economic resources of an area, but also the literature, by creating new legends and forbidding the telling of the old, he could, in a short period, replace the old "history" with an entirely new one simply because nobody told the old stories anymore.

Besides, his subjects had a motive for accepting this new "literature." With a few notable exceptions, conquered nations gained more than they lost by being subject to the Inca empire. The Inca rulers brought stability, plentiful food, and protection from marauders. That being the case, the new subjects probably wanted to believe the legends of the Incas, because their own legends and gods, created in a pre-Inca age of want and warfare, now seemed to offer nothing. Such legends could be forgotten in a generation.

THE CREATION
OF MANKIND

In the very beginning, there was nothing but a dark sky over a great lake—Lake Titicaco. Deep within the lake lived the god Viracocha and his wife, Mamacocha, the goddess of the rain and the wind.

After many years, Viracocha became lonely and asked his wife how he might overcome this feeling.

Mamacocha, who was very wise, suggested that he create a group of human beings to worship him.

"Out of what should I make these creatures?" asked Viracocha, and Mamacocha told him to make them out of stone and breathe life into them.

Before he could create the people themselves, Viracocha had to make a place for them to live. So he gathered up mounds of mud from the bottom of Lake Titicaco and piled it up to create the mountains, plains,

and valleys of the earth. That done he took stone and shaped it into people. But because the earth was dark and he could not see what he was doing, the creatures he made were ugly, misshapen, and too large. He also erred by making only males. And as if that weren't enough, the creatures were very stupid. When he tried to teach them to worship him, they could not remember the ceremonies, and they kept dropping the sacred objects. Dissatisfied with his creations, Viracocha destroyed them all and became depressed.

"Well, try again, my husband!" said Mamacocha, who was a little disgruntled by her husband's lack of originality and inability to get the job done right.

This time, however, Viracocha, who really had an artistic temperament, decided to go somewhere else to create humans, to a place where he might get fresh inspiration. He traveled to Tiahuanaco and built a great palace out of the huge stones he found there. Then, so that he could more easily see what he was making, he created the sun, and to help him know how long he had worked, he created the moon to measure the passage of days.

After making all these things, he felt more comfortable with the act of creation, and he once again took stones in hand to create a group of humans. This time, however, he made two kinds, male and female, so that each could make the other happy. He sculpted some women pregnant and some holding babies—to save him the work of making more of these creatures later—and a few with no babies at all. He also painted their clothes and gave some long hair and some short hair, so that there would be some way to immediately tell the difference between classes; otherwise, some low-caste men might presume to privileges that were not truly theirs.

When he had created a large number of these creatures, he took them down underground with him and distributed them inside many caves. Then, finally, he breathed life into them so they came to life and walked out of the caves into the world, which is why people from all the tribes in South America share the belief that they originally came from caves in the ground.

After he was done with the creation of humankind, Viracocha was satisfied for a time. He decided to leave his creations alone for a time, to give them a chance to develop, but soon he became curious and set forth to discover what had become of them.

Viracocha went forth from Lake Titicaco in the guise of an old man with long hair and a beard, carrying a gnarled staff, and wearing an old cloak. For protection, he carried a bag

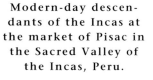

Modern-day descendants of the Incas at the market of Pisac in the Sacred Valley of the Incas, Peru.

of thunderbolts. When he had traveled fifty miles (80km), he came to the first group of people he had created, the Canan people. These people did not recognize him, but saw only a helpless old man, and they ran forward to rob and kill him.

Viracocha stopped, reached into his bag, and pulled out a thunderbolt. He threw the bolt against a mountainside, and all the trees and plants caught fire. Soon, the Canan people saw a wall of flame where there had been a green hillside only moments before. Realizing they were in the presence of a truly powerful creature, they dropped to the ground and crawled toward him, wailing and begging forgiveness. Their fear pleased Viracocha—he waved his staff and the fire died out.

He then told the Cana that he was their creator. But because they had attempted to do him harm, he demanded that they build a great temple in his honor and fill it with gold and silver. When they had done this, Viracocha forgave them and resumed his journey.

The next group of people he came to were the Urcos, who recognized him immediately and came forward to praise him. He was quite pleased by this peaceful reception, especially when the Urcos asked if they might build him a golden throne for him to rest on awhile. He told them that would be appropriate, and when it was done, he sat, rested, and talked to the people.

After leaving the Urcos, he kept walking north until he came to the present site of Cuzco, which was not yet a city. The people welcomed him with such warmth and affection that he told them that someday he would send them a great and benevolent ruler to watch over them.

From Cuzco he went on to visit all of his creations until he came to a village near the sea where there lived a beautiful maiden named Cahuillaca. Everyone who saw her wanted to sleep with her, but she had decreed

that she would give herself only to a great man. Viracocha decided to teach her a lesson in humility.

One day, as Cahuillaca sat weaving beneath a tree, Viracocha changed himself into a bird. He perched on a branch next to the fruit of the tree and deposited some of his sperm on the fruit. Later, Cahuillaca grew thirsty and reached up to pluck the fruit from the tree. When she ate it, she unwittingly took Viracocha's sperm into her.

A modern inhabitant of Cuzco spins llama wool into thread.

A woman, her child,
and a llama on a
ridge above Cuzco.

In a few months it became obvious that she was pregnant, which was strange as she and everyone else in the village knew that she was a virgin. In nine months she gave birth to a fine, healthy boy, but she still did not know how or by whom she had become pregnant. Finally, some months later, she called all the men of the village together and demanded that the one responsible for her pregnancy admit it. Of course, all the men of the village claimed to be the father so that they might claim the beautiful girl as their own. After a few minutes of this, Cahuillaca became disgusted with the noise of so many men claiming her as a bride. She stamped her foot and screamed for silence. Then she said to her baby, "Child, go forth and find your father!" She then set the baby on the ground, and it began to crawl among the assembled men.

All this time Viracocha was standing on the outside of the circle of men that surrounded Cahuillaca. Of all the men there, he was the only one dressed in rags; the rest were in their finest clothes. The baby crawled among the feet of the men, making straight for Viracocha. When it reached the ragged old man, the infant clutched at his legs. Viracocha bent down and picked the child up. Cahuillaca was horrified.

"What?" she exclaimed. "You horrid, dirty old man. You could not possibly be the father of so fine a child. I would be ashamed to be your wife!" She ran up to Viracocha, grabbed the child from his arms, and ran away. Too late for Cahuillaca to see, Viracocha threw off his ragged old cloak and revealed himself in a bright golden cloak such as only gods wear. Fearing to lose the beautiful girl, he chased after her. But he did not catch her.

Desperate to find her, Viracocha raced on, until he came upon a condor eating a dead rabbit. "Have you seen a beautiful woman with a baby?" he asked the bird. The condor flew high into the air, saw the maid, and flew back to earth. "Keep straight ahead, Viracocha, and you will find her."

"Thank you, noblest of birds," said Viracocha. "You will be the luckiest of birds, and will eat all manner of flesh so that you will become larger than any other bird. Also, if any human raises a hand against you, he will have bad luck for the rest of his life."

Viracocha plunged on, but he soon became confused again. He stopped a passing skunk and asked, "Have you seen a woman with a baby?" But the skunk, who always went around with its nose to the ground, had not seen her. "I have seen nothing, great Viracocha." The god became angry and proclaimed, "You will always stink, and men will hate you, and all the other animals will run from you so you will never have any friends!"

Next, he met a mountain lion and asked the lion if it had seen the woman with the baby. The lion, who had been sitting on a high branch so that it could see far in every direction, said, "Yes, great Viracocha, I have seen the woman. She is just ahead of you."

"Thank you, great cat. You will be the most renowned of all creatures on the land. Men will honor you and prize your skin in their most sacred ceremonies. You will eat only the best animals and so grow both large and strong."

Next he came to some parrots perched on a low branch. "Have you seen a woman with a baby?" But the parrots had seen nothing because they were busy talking to each other and were not paying attention to the things around them.

"Curse you, silly birds!" cried Viracocha. "From this day on, you will be able to speak only what men teach you to say, and they will teach you silly words and phrases so that all who meet you will laugh at you."

After that, Viracocha hurried on, periodically stopping to ask directions from one animal or another. Those who helped him were rewarded with skills and gifts, but those who gave him no encouragement were cursed in various ways: the fox became sneaky and the turtle slow, while the hawk became a bold hunter who was honored above all other birds except the condor.

Viracocha walked all the way to where the land meets the sea, but he could not find Cahuillaca. Exhausted, he stopped to consider what he should do next. He could go back, he thought, but he had already seen all there was to see on land. Ahead lay the great sea, and perhaps the beautiful mother of his young son. He pulled his beautiful cloak from his

Just as the Maya and Aztec artists excelled in feather work, so did the Inca. This hat, made between A.D. 1570 and 1630, is decorated with white and tan feathers.

shoulders, stretched it over the water to make a raft, and set out to the west, promising himself that he would someday return to look upon his creations once again.

HOW THE INCAS LEARNED TO BE CIVILIZED

After the creation of humankind, the Sun god Viracocha (although some say it was Viracocha's father, Inti) decided that mankind was without aim or purpose. Humans wandered the earth without clothing, eating wild plants, small animals, and even other people. They mated indiscriminately so that no son knew who his father was. Without leadership, Viracocha/Inti believed, mankind would always be unhappy and would remain little better than an animal.

So Viracocha or Inti looked around to see if there was not one group of people, among all those inhabiting the world, who had the charisma and special abilities to make them good leaders for all the rest of humankind.

Near the site where Cuzco would one day stand, Viracocha found a very small tribe that showed promise: the Ayar. This tribe was so small that it had only eight people in it—four brothers and their four sisters—but they were very intelligent. They were so smart, in fact, that they had learned, without the aid of any god, to build crude huts for themselves and to make clothes out of leaves. They had even begun to understand that plants grew from tiny seeds, though they had not yet discovered agriculture.

Although this tribe had potential, there was a problem. The leader of the tribe, Ayar Cachi, was a strong, willful, and intemperate man who sometimes took out his anger on his

brothers and sisters by beating them. At other times, he threw giant stones around the countryside, creating great gouges in the hills and making such loud noises that all the animals were scared away and the tribe went hungry because they could not find meat.

The other three brothers—Manco Capac, Ayar Oco, and Ayar Ayca—and one of the sisters, Mama Occlo, wanted to do something about their loud and destructive brother. Each made many suggestions, but finally Mama Occlo came up with the best idea. The great weakness of Ayar Cachi, she said, was his

pride, and all they had to do was to use this pride against him. She quickly outlined her plan, and Manco Capac, the bravest brother, volunteered to set it in motion.

A few days later, Manco Capac said to Ayar Cachi, "My brother, there is a beautiful llama in a cave. He is the grandest creature I have ever seen, but I am too weak to pull him from the cave. Perhaps you, with your great strength, can drag him from the cave."

"You are a weak and spindly creature, Manco Capac, if you cannot pull a llama from a hole in the ground. Show me where it is and I will get the llama, and then I shall come back and beat you for your cowardice and weakness."

Of course, there was no llama, but Manco Capac led Ayar Cachi to the mouth of a deep cave in a deep valley, and with no hesitation Ayar Cachi went down into it. No sooner had he descended into the dark than Manco Capac, Ayar Cachi, Ayar Oco, and Mama Occlo rushed to the opening and filled the mouth with stones. They then climbed the high mountains on either side of the cave's entrance and pushed these giant peaks into the

valley so that the cave was covered with tons of rock. Try as he might, even the powerful Ayar Cachi could not escape, and to this day he is still in the cave, which is located only twenty miles (32km) from Cuzco, deep underneath a level plain. Every once in awhile, Ayar Cachi tries to escape, roaring and shaking the earth, as he tries to find a way out. This is why there have always been so many earthquakes in Peru and Ecuador.

Viracocha, who had seen the whole thing, was impressed, for he knew that great strength is not as powerful as the wisdom Mama Occlo had shown in creating the plan or the courage that Manco Capac had shown in carrying the plan out. Right then Viracocha decided he had found the people to teach the people of the earth all they needed to know to be happy and prosperous.

So Viracocha called Manco Capac and Mama Occlo to him, saying: "You will be the instrument that I will use to help civilize the people of the world. Now they are dirty, hungry, and stupid because they live like animals. They wear no clothes, they mate with each other like dogs, and they eat whatever they can find on the ground. I will teach you everything about growing plants, building houses, making weapons, and weaving cloth. You will teach all people these things, and when they have learned these things they will be happy. You must teach them to work together, to share what they make with one another, and to worship me for giving them these things.

When you have done this, I will make you rulers over the people so that you and your descendants can make certain that people will always do what I have decreed."

Viracocha continued, "I also want you to build me a great city where I will be worshiped and from which you will rule. So that you may know where to build that city I give you this golden rod that is as long as a man's arm and as thick as two fingers. After you start on your journey to educate the people, stop at dusk to make camp. Before you settle in for the night, drive this rod into the ground. When you find a place where you can stick the rod its own length into the ground, there you will build my city, which you will call Cuzco—The Navel of the World—for Cuzco will be the source of a new life for the people of the world."

After the god had taught Manco Capac and Mama Occlo all the arts of civilization, they set forth to teach and rule the world.

When they made camp the first night, they thrust the golden rod into the ground, just as they had been ordered. But it went in only a few inches (cm), so they knew they were not at the right place. The place where they first camped was twenty-four miles (38km) south of Cuzco and was called Caparec Tempu—The Morning Place.

The next day, the couple reached the Valley of Cuzco, and that night, after they made camp, they again stuck the rod into the earth. To their amazement, it disappeared completely from view. The place where this happened was named Huanacauri, The Place of the Rainbow, because it was a place of great promise.

OPPOSITE: This depiction of Coya Mama, the wife of Manco Capac, the last Inca ruler, shows her holding a mirror reflecting the sun; this mirror represents her husband as the descendent of the sun.

LEFT: The silver statue of a nobleman. These figures with gold, stone, and pink shell inlay were frequently dressed up in tiny clothes and placed among the wrappings of a mummy. Note the elongated ear lobes— a sign of nobility among the Incas.

Unhappily, the Valley of Cuzco was inhabited by fierce people who did not want to be civilized, and they ran out carrying rocks with which to kill Manco Capac and Mama Occlo.

But Mama Occlo killed the first attacker with a sling, slit open his chest, ripped out his lungs, and inflated them into a bloody balloon. This gruesome action so terrified the people that they stopped in their tracks, threw themselves on the ground, and begged for forgiveness.

After the battle, Manco Capac and Mama Occlo gathered the people together and announced their commission from Viracocha. The people were easily convinced that these two truly had something valuable to teach them, for their clothes were magnificent and they wore large golden disks in their earlobes. The disks impressed everyone the most, and so Manco Capac announced that those who proved especially worthy would be rewarded by the right to wear earlobe plugs.

To begin their teaching, brother and sister divided the people into males and females.

Manco Capac taught the men what foods were the most nutritious, whether they were grain crops, fruits, or vegetables, then taught them how to pick the best seeds, how to make hoes, and how to build irrigation ditches to bring water from the mountains to the valley. He taught them how to build terraces into the mountainsides and how to bring fertile soil from the valley floors to increase the area of land available for growing crops. He showed them how to skin animals, tan the leather, and make sandals so that they would not bruise their feet. Finally, knowing that as soon as the people of the valley grew wealthy with crops, others would want to steal from them, Manco Capac taught the men how to make weapons: clubs, slings, bolos, lances, and bows and arrows. He then taught them the arts of war, and with a small army he conquered all the people for twenty-four miles (38.4km) to the west, twenty-seven miles (43.2km) to the south, twelve miles (19.2km) to the east, and twenty miles (32km) to the north. But many tribes joined the Incas without fighting, for they saw the wealth and the powerful army of the people of Cuzco and wanted to share in this life.

Meanwhile, Mama Occlo taught the women how to build looms, weave cotton into cloth, and finally to make the cloth into clothes. She also explained how to build houses and how to group these dwellings into villages for protection.

After seven years, Manco Capac and Mama Occlo sent out people from the Valley of Cuzco to tell others what they had learned. These people were dressed in the most beautiful clothes so that their words would carry more power, for what man or woman standing naked would not envy and respect those who wear beautiful, warm clothing? In this way, the knowledge of the Incas was spread from group to group, and civilization was brought to many.

THE VIRGIN OF
THE SUN AND
THE SHEPHERD

In Cuzco, in the Aclla-huaci, the Convent of the Sun Virgins, there once lived a beautiful maiden named Chuguillanto. When she was seven years old, this maiden had been selected from among all the girls of her tribe because she was so beautiful. She was so lovely that birds who saw her stopped their singing, for their beautiful songs were nothing compared to this girl. Furthermore, she was without blemish of any kind: her skin did not have so much as the smallest mole or even freckle on it. Her hair was the color of gold, and it was this characteristic, among all the other perfect ones, that dictated her special position in the Aclla-huaci. Because her hair was like the sun, the emperor had decided that she should be saved as a special offering to the Sun god in case a human sacrifice was ever needed to appease that god. The Incas did not sacrifice hu-

man beings as readily as the Maya and Aztecs to the west. Only great disasters or famine could call forth the supreme sacrifice, and even then the Incas would sacrifice only a few people.

So Chuquillanto lived in the Aclla-huaci with four thousand other maidens, waiting for the day when she would be sacrificed for the good of her country. Most of the other girls were there for a different reason, for only the most perfect and beautiful, like Chuquillanto, were reserved for sacrifice. Some maidens were designated as companions for the emperor should he occasionally tire of his wife; others were set aside as wives for Inca nobles who had especially pleased the emperor. Still others were in training to learn how to serve the sacred mummies of past emperors—to dress and wash them, and to sit by these ancient corpses carefully flicking away the flies that seemed always to be near.

To learn their respective tasks, the maidens had daily sessions with the female guardians of the Aclla-huaci. At night, before

These modern Inca women hold plates of maize to offer to the Sun God Inti.

going to bed, they all bathed. Because it was believed that the skin of a woman remained at its softest when washed in the water of her home province, each girl would wash using water that had flowed all the way from her homeland through a complicated series of channels and pipes, which were often hundreds of miles (km) long.

In the late afternoon, after the girls learned their lessons and before they took their baths, the guards of the Aclla-huaci allowed the Sun Virgins to leave the convent and wander where they wished. It may seem strange that the virgins were allowed this freedom, but the penalty for losing one's virginity to anyone but the emperor or a chosen noble was so harsh that nobody dreamed that a girl would risk it: a Sun Virgin who engaged in sex was buried alive and her partner was hanged by his feet until the blood collected

in his head and his brain burst. If the man was already married, his wife and children were also killed, along with every living soul in his village.

The Sun Virgins were never allowed outside the Aclla-huaci alone—they always traveled in pairs, and when they returned, they were separated and each was questioned closely as to the details of their outing. Should their stories differ, the guards investigated the discrepancy carefully to see if there had been an opportunity for one of the girls to have lost her virginity during her absence. The emperor bragged that a deflowered girl was always discovered through such questionings, and it was a point of honor that no girl who had lost her virginity had ever escaped detection or punishment.

The guards also checked the girls for any love charms, for among the Incas a love

Remains of Incas and their grave goods found recently in Chiclayo, Peru. Modern grave robbers have done great damage to important archaeological sites in their search for gold.

charm was considered proof of intimate relations between a man and a woman. If a maiden tried to sneak any such thing into the Aclla-huaci, she was immediately buried alive and soldiers were sent to find the man who had given her the charm and punish him according to custom. These precautions were considered enough to protect the Sun Virgins.

One day Chuquillanto and another Sun Virgin wandered farther than they ever had before. The girls saw a herd of llamas and, lying in the shade of a tree, a handsome young shepherd. The two girls, thinking to have some fun, sneaked up to the boy and stood before him as he slept. Their perfumes drifted down to his nose, and he slowly woke up to see two of the most beautiful women he had ever seen. All the girls of his village were deeply tanned from their long days in the fields. Their hands and feet were rough from hard work. They smelled of smoke, grease, and guinea pig fat from preparing meals. And most had fleas and lice.

Dazed with sleep and the beauty of the maidens, the boy thought he was in the presence of goddesses. He sprang to his feet and immediately fell to his knees. The girls laughed at his confusion, swore that they were not goddesses, and asked him to rise. They asked him his name, and he told them it was Acoynapa. The three young people then sat down beneath a tree, ate some chuno (dehydrated potato), and drank a little chicha that Acoynapa had left over from lunch.

Chuquillanto noticed that Acoynapa wore a silver *campu*, or pendant, on a small sil-

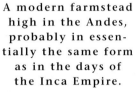
A modern farmstead high in the Andes, probably in essentially the same form as in the days of the Inca Empire.

ver chain around his forehead. This pretty charm sparkled in the sunlight, and Chuquillanto asked to see it more closely. Acoynapa leaned forward to give her a better view and was overcome by Chuquillanto's closeness. He quickly drew back, for he felt himself falling in love with her and knew that dreadful punishment awaited them both if he yielded to his feelings.

"I will give you my silver campu if you like," the boy declared.

But Chuquillanto said no, for they would both be slain if a guard found the campu when the girls returned to the Aclla-huaci. So the three talked until dusk, and then Chuquillanto and her companion returned to the Aclla-huaci.

All night Chuquillanto thought about Acoynapa. She knew she was in love, and she weighed that feeling against the punishment she knew awaited her if she gave into her emotions. Being a practical girl, she decided to try and ignore her feelings, but also determined that there was no harm in seeing the boy again as long as she took her companion with her.

During the same night, Acoynapa also tossed and turned. He loved the girl and was willing to risk anything for her, but he also knew the penalty for sleeping with Chuquillanto. He had no desire to hang by his heels in the village square while all his neighbors stood round waiting for blood to gush out of his eyes, ears, and nose, but neither could he

Comparatively few wooden artifacts have survived from the Inca period. This is a wooden vase used to hold offerings of maize. The design is of a woman harvesting crops, probably potatoes.

get the beautiful maiden out of his mind. He slept little, and in the morning he awoke feeling sick and weak.

His mother found him in a terrible state and was frightened when his condition got worse throughout the day. At first, he would not say what was causing his problem, but she gradually wormed it out of him.

When Acoynapa told his mother about his feelings, she tried every argument to persuade him to forget the girl. For a time, it seemed that the boy might heed his mother's good advice, but the next morning he was again sick. This continued for a week, and it finally became clear that the love sickness, accompanied by a lack of interest in any food, would soon result in his death. His mother was torn between the certainty that the boy would die if he did not gain Chuquillanto's love and the real possibility that if he succeeded in gaining that love he would be killed according to the edict of the emperor.

Now this lady was not just any Inca mother—she was renowned throughout the Valley of Cuzco for her magical talents. People came to her for help with sickness, to find lost objects, and for aid in conceiving children.

"I would be a fine mother if I let my son die when I have helped so many other people with their problems," thought the woman, and she quickly devised a plan. Her son could not enjoy any intimacy with Chuquillanto when the girl was outside the Aclla-huaci, for either the girl's companion would report the transgression or the careful questionings of the guards at the gate would find her out.

Therefore it would be necessary to get her son into the Aclla-huaci. Once inside, Acoynapa might be able to sleep with the girl, for nobody thought it necessary to guard the girls after they passed the gates. The mother hoped that, with his lust satisfied, Acoynapa would get over his love sickness and be able to return to a normal life.

If the guards somehow discovered that Chuquillanto was no longer a virgin, the blame would fall on somebody else, for Chuquillanto's companion could truthfully testify that nothing had happened outside the Aclla-huaci when she had talked with Acoynapa. All this was rather cold-blooded of the mother—she did not care if Chuquillanto was discovered as long as her son recovered.

But how could they get the boy inside the Aclla-huaci? Like all good sorceresses, the mother had a collection of magic potions, objects, and animal parts. From this collection

A modern Inca reenacting the Raymi Festival. This festival—which was held four times each year, in June, September, October, and December—began with the ritual drinking of chicha to bring on a mild intoxication; this was followed by a ritual dance and chanting. All of this produced a mild hypnosis during which the participants experienced ecstatic visions.

she selected a magic staff that not only was beautifully carved and very strong, but also had the power to carry a person inside it—using certain chants and spells, a person could actually become thin enough to enter the staff. Then, using other magic chants, the person could leave the staff. She took the staff into her son's bedroom, where the boy lay half dead, and explained her plan to him. His health instantly improved.

Now while all this had been going on, Chuquillanto had been wandering the countryside searching for Acoynapa. She realized that to make love to the young man was impossible, but she wanted desperately to see him again anyway. She and her companion wandered about, asking for the house of Acoynapa, until they finally found it. They knocked at the door and entered. Chuquillanto asked for Acoynapa, and his mother replied that the boy was dead. Chuquillanto fell to the floor and rolled about in misery. This was good, thought the mother, for Chuquillanto's companion would report the incident—and no suspicion could attach itself to a dead man.

When the girl's wails subsided a little, Acoynapa's mother said, "I grieve for you, my child, but there is nothing I can do. Let me give you something to remember my child by. Here is his favorite walking staff. Take it and remember my son."

Of course, Acoynapa was already concealed in the staff. The virgins returned to Cuzco, and at the gate to the Aclla-huaci, the guards inspected the two maidens. They did not think to refuse the girl the right to take the staff inside, for it was just a stick, not a love charm, and the man who had carved it was dead. What harm could there be?

That night, Chuquillanto went to bed clutching the staff to her. As she lay there in the dark, she heard the voice of her beloved calling her. She jumped up, lit a lamp, and saw Acoynapa lying in bed beside her. Overjoyed, the two enjoyed each other's company all night long.

The next morning, Chuquillanto awoke, put the staff in a corner, and went about her business. In the afternoon she took the staff with her when she and her companion went out, and that night she returned with the staff to another night of lovemaking. It seemed the perfect arrangement.

But then fate intervened. Famine struck the empire, and many people died. This calamity was quickly succeeded by a deadly plague, and soon the roads and villages were filled with corpses that nobody had the strength to bury.

The emperor consulted his wise men and was told that it was time for a sacrifice. At the Aclla-huaci, all knew that Chuquillanto would be the victim, and everyone was happy for her. To die so for the emperor was to live eternally in bliss with the Sun god. There was not even any pain in the sacrifice. The victim was drugged with a special mixture of chicha so that she was insensible by the time the priest drew the cord tightly around her neck

and strangled her. Only then was her head struck off and her heart torn out. It was considered a privilege and an honor to die in this manner.

But the Sun god would accept only the purest of victims—a woman without blemish either inside or out. It went without saying that the victim had to be a virgin. To offer a tainted sacrifice would be blasphemy, and the gods would surely punish an emperor who did such a thing. Ignorance about the victim's virginity was no excuse. Misery would surely be compounded on the whole empire for so impious an act.

Chuquillanto, knowing that she was no longer acceptable as a sacrifice, did not know what to do. To admit she was not a virgin would only get her and her beloved killed. And to submit herself to the priests would bring further misery to the entire empire.

Desperate, the two lovers decided to flee. Perhaps, they thought, they could escape into the mysterious jungles to the east. There were legends and rumors that the Chiriguano, who constantly raided the eastern border of the Inca land, occasionally welcomed refugees from the empire.

With this risky plan in mind, Chuquillanto left the Aclla-huaci for the last time, tightly clutching the staff that held her lover. As they reached the top of the mountain pass at the border of the Empire at Challapampa, however, the gods turned them both into stone pillars, one on either side of the road leading into the jungle. And those pillars stand there to this day, twin piles of rock flanking the road to freedom. The two lovers will spend all eternity facing freedom side by side, but they are neither free nor really together. Whether the gods did this in homage to their great love for each other or as revenge for breaking the laws of the empire is still hotly debated each night by the peasants who sit huddled round the fire drinking chicha.

The old Inca trails still wind through the mountains of Peru. Here in the Urahamba River Valley, a trail follows along the course of the river.

HOW
THE MYTHS
HAVE CHANGED

Myths seldom die—they just change and adapt. It is a big leap from the myth of King Arthur as it was first told among the ancient Celts of Wales, sometime before A.D. 500, to the King Arthur of *Monty Python and the Holy Grail*, written in A.D. 1975, but ultimately the two myths are the same.

So it is with the ancient myths of Mesoamerica and modern Peru, for the old myths of the Aztecs, Maya, and Incas did not die when the Spanish invaded;

Today many of the old myths survive as tales of heroes and saints. This Guatemalan farmer surveys the wares at a roadside stand—an odd assortment of saints' images and masks that resemble the mythological beings found on ancient Maya buildings.

103

they just changed. Following the European conquest, the telling of the old stories was forbidden, for the Catholic Church viewed this as heresy. So secretly, the myth tellers simply altered the stories they told in such a way as to fool the meddlesome priest, but not so drastically that the native listeners would not recognize them.

On the most basic level, the storytellers stopped using the names of the old gods and substituted innocuous names like the "Ancient One" or used noncontroversial names like "Sun" and "Moon." Sometimes, the myth tellers even borrowed elements from the Christians, much like Christianity borrowed from the old pagan religions that had come before. Perhaps, thought the storytellers, the local priest might even be fooled into thinking that the "simple" natives were merely adapting Bible stories.

Today, although many of these tales are still told, the people of Mexico, Guatemala, Honduras, and Peru are rapidly being brought into the twentieth century. In time, as their society changes even more, the myths these people tell will undoubtedly again have to change or be lost.

THE AZTEC FLOOD MYTH

One mythological tale that seems to be common to many different religions from around the world is the story of the flood. It figures prominently in the Christian tradition and the myths of the ancient Greeks, and the Nahua of Central America—descendants of the Aztecs who live in the modern Mexican states of Guererro and Vera Cruz—also tell of a great flood in which all the land of the world was submerged. Historians know that the Nahua flood myth predates the arrival of the Spanish because there are references to it in glyph books that have survived from the time of the Aztecs. From studying these books, it is clear that the only change the

myth tellers made for the benefit of their Catholic rulers was to incorporate the ark into their ancient tale and change the name of their supreme god to the "Ancient One."

Eons ago, the Ancient One became unhappy with mankind for not honoring him appropriately, and he decided to destroy them all. But at the last minute, he decided to save one man, along with his wife and children, because they were such hard workers.

"Certainly," said the Ancient One to himself, "if I decide to rebuild the world later, it would be good to have such hard workers to help me."

So the Ancient One went to this family and said, "You need to stop working in the maize field and do what I tell you because I am going to destroy all the people in the world except for you."

Then he told them to find the biggest cedar tree in the forest, cut it down and hollow out a huge canoe, then fill the canoe with food and water—for soon the Ancient One would make it rain harder than it had ever rained before, and the family needed a boat or they would surely drown.

In a few days, after much hard work, the canoe was ready. That night, the family crawled into the boat and pulled mats over the top to keep out the rain. At dusk the rain started, and just before dawn the man felt the canoe lurch. He looked out from under the mats and saw that the boat had broken loose from the ground and was floating! All day the family watched the water rise, and by nightfall their craft was floating among the branches of the highest trees.

They ate some food and went to sleep. When they woke the next morning, there was nothing but water as far as the eye could see. They floated for days, and before long they had eaten all their food and drunk all their water.

When they were near starvation, however, the Ancient One remembered them and ordered the water to go down. The waters of the earth went back into their natural streams, lakes, and oceans. But many of the world's fish did not make it, and the ground was covered with dead fish.

The man picked up some fish and ate them. Then he decided that he would build a fire to cook them. But the Ancient One came to him and said, "Do not build a fire." When the Ancient One disappeared, however, the woman and children began to cry and wail for a fire to cook the fish, so the man disobeyed his god.

When the Ancient One smelled the smoke and the delicious odor of cooked fish, he came to the family in an ugly mood. "How

Statues of Tlaloc, the rain god—a deity the Maya and Aztec shared—are usually made with goggly eyes and large teeth. He supposedly lived in caves high in the mountains.

dare you disobey me? You are just as disobedient and difficult as all the other people who drowned!"

So the Ancient One changed the man and his wife into stupid monkeys who sat all day and chattered about nothing. He changed the children to buzzards and ordered them to eat all the dead animals that were left over from the flood. Then the Ancient One made new and better people.

WHY THE PIG HAS SMALL EARS, A FLAT NOSE, AND A CURLY TAIL: A MAYA MYTH

The most popular myth of the Maya was the story of how Hunahpu and Xbalanque defeated the lords of the underworld. Of course, that myth was so well known that even the Spanish had heard of it, but there were other tales about these brave and resourceful brothers that were less well known, and the myth tellers could tell these stories without fear of discovery and so remember and honor their old way of life. To be completely safe, however, the storytellers did not use the names of the two heroes, for they knew that any Maya who heard the story would know who they were really were.

One day, four brothers went hunting in the woods. Two of the brothers were lean and quick, but the other two were fat and greedy; also, the four young men weren't true brothers, for they had the same mother but the lean and quick brothers had a different father from the fat and greedy ones.

Two Maya boys from the village of Cancuc in Chiapas, Mexico.

As the four marched through the woods, they came to a great fruit tree. Each brother wanted some of the fruit, but the fat and greedy brothers, who had seen the tree first, climbed up and would not let the others join them. The lean and quick brothers stood around the base of the tree and begged for some good fruit, but their half-brothers threw down only seeds, skin, and rinds.

Finally, one of the lean and quick brothers had an idea. Using the magic he had learned from his grandmother, he gathered up the remains of the fruit, molded the pieces together in the shape of a gopher, and breathed life into it. He then set the gopher on the ground, and it began to chew through the roots of the fruit tree so that it fell to the ground, knocking the fat and greedy brothers unconscious.

The magician brother then ran home and begged some tortillas from his mother. When he returned to the spot where his siblings lay, he tore the tortillas into pieces and molded the soft bread into little round ears, flat noses, and straight thin tails. He then stuck these things onto the bodies of his unconscious brothers. When the fat and greedy boys woke up, they took one look at each other and ran screaming into the woods. As the cursed boys ran by, however, the lean and quick brothers grabbed their tails and twisted them. And that is why the pig has small ears, a flat nose, and a curly tail.

Maya woman from San Christobal, Chiapas, Mexico. The pig she has with her is not a pet— it's just that walking the animal is the most practical way to get it home.

HOW THE
CONDOR
TURNED BLACK

A great number of Indian myths that are still told today required no change and no subterfuge on the part of the tellers. These stories are so innocent that not even the intolerant Spanish friars could object to them. Today, these tales are probably told in much the same way they were before the Spanish conquest.

Once upon a time, a great condor, resplendent in his cool white mantle of feathers, was flying grandly over a meadow. In that meadow was a beautiful young maiden guarding a flock of sheep. Observing the maiden's beauty, the condor immediately flew down to talk to her. When the girl saw the great bird, however, she ran screaming into a nearby cave, and the condor realized he needed to change himself into a handsome young man if he was not to frighten the girl.

The next day, the bird confronted the girl in the shape of a man. He talked sweetly to her, and she thought he was very funny and clever. He was funniest when he tried to scratch his back, for he said he had a terrible itch between his shoulder blades. But wiggle and squirm as he might, he didn't seem able to reach the spot.

The girl watched for a while, and although it was amusing to see the man try and scratch himself, she felt sorry for him and offered to help him relieve his suffering.

The man turned his back to the girl and bent down, for he was too tall for the girl to reach the itch. As soon as the condor felt her touch the spot between his shoulder blades, however, he changed immediately back into a bird and flew high in the air with the girl on his back.

At first she was terrified, but then the novelty of the adventure and the grandeur of the view calmed her. As the condor soared higher and higher, she thought that it might not be a bad thing to marry the bird. When he took her to his cave high in the Andes to meet his mother, his father, and his condor brothers and sisters, they were so kind to her that she accepted his proposal of marriage. That night, when she enjoyed the embraces of the condor, she was certain she had made the right choice.

But the next morning she awoke and was hungry. She asked the condor for something to eat, and he immediately flew down into the valleys and brought back a tapir that had been dead for only a few days. It smelled bad and was bloated with gases, just the way condors like their meat. But the dead tapir made the girl sick.

"Maybe if it were cooked it wouldn't smell so bad and make me sick," said the girl.

So the condor brought her wood for a fire and a piece of burning coal from a farmer's hearth to cook the meat with. Once she had cooked the tapir, it didn't taste too bad, and for a time she was happy. She soon became pregnant and began to lay eggs. She even started to grow feathers. But she soon grew tired of sitting on a bird's nest dressed in only a few feathers.

One day, when the condor and his whole family were away hunting, loneliness overcame the girl and she began to cry. "It is so cold here," she sobbed. "I can hardly keep myself warm, let alone these eggs. I'm sorry I ever came here!"

Just then, to her great surprise, a parrot landed in the cave and said to her, "I've been waiting for the condor and his family to leave so I could speak with you. Your mother misses you very much and wants you to come home. I promised her I would find you and offer to bring you back if you wished to return."

"Oh please, please take me home, parrot! I'm so cold and hungry."

With that, the girl climbed on the parrot's back (parrots were much larger birds then) and soon arrived home.

The girl's mother greeted her with hugs and kisses, even though the girl looked silly with her skinny frame and the few paltry feathers about her. She also smelled bad because of all the dead meat she had been eating. But a few days of good food and several baths fixed her up, and the girl quickly returned to a normal life.

In a few days, however, the great condor appeared at her door.

"Come home, wife, I miss you. My brothers and sisters miss you, too. The eggs are beginning to hatch, for mother has been sitting on them since you left."

But the girl screamed and threw a pot at him, and the great bird flew away. That night, his sorrow was so great that his feathers turned from snowy white to deepest black. And that is why the condor is black.

A classic Andean Condor, an animal revered by the ancient and modern Incas for its strength and intelligence. A modern condor can have a wing span of ten feet (3m) and can soar for hours at higher than five thousand feet (1,524m) without flapping its wings. Condors do not build nests—they simply lay their eggs on rocky crags.

BIBLIOGRAPHY

Bernand, Carmen. *The Incas: People of the Sun*. New York: Harry N. Abrams, 1994.

Bierhorst, John. *Black Rainbow: Legends of the Incas and Myths of Ancient Peru*. New York: Farrar, Straus & Giroux, 1976.

_____. *The Mythology of Mexico and Central America*. New York: William Morrow & Co., 1990.

Boone, Elizabeth H., ed. *Ritual Human Sacrifice in Mesoamerica*. Washington, D.C.: Dumbarton Oaks Research Library and Collections, 1984.

Bray, Warwick. *Everyday Life of the Aztecs*. New York: Dorset Press, 1987.

Cameron, Ian. *Kingdom of the Sun God: A History of the Andes and Their People*. New York: Facts on File, 1990.

Carrasco, David. *Religions of Mesoamerica*. Chicago: University of Chicago Press, 1990.

Coe, Michael D. *The Maya*. 5th ed. London: Thames and Hudson, 1993.

_____. *Mexico*. London: Thames and Hudson, 1984.

_____. *Mexico from the Olmecs to the Aztecs*. London: Thames and Hudson, 1962.

Davies, Nigel. *The Incas*. Boulder, Colo.: University of Colorado Press, 1994.

Fash, William L. *Scribes, Warriors and Kings: The City of Copan and the Ancient Maya*. London: Thames and Hudson, 1991.

Freidel, David, Linda Schele, and Joy Parker. *Maya Cosmos: 3000 Years on the Shaman's Path*. New York: William Morrow & Co., 1993.

Gillespie, Susan D. *The Aztec Kings*. Tucson, Ariz.: University of Arizona Press, 1994.

Jennings, Gary. *Aztec*. New York: Atheneum Publishers, 1980.

Kendall, Ann. *Everyday Life of the Incas*. London: Dorset Press, 1989.

Leon-Portilla, Miguel. *The Broken Spears: The Aztec Account of the Conquest of Mexico*. Boston: Beacon Press, 1990.

Marrin, Albert. *Inca and Spaniard: Pizarro and the Conquest of Peru*. New York: Atheneum Publishers, 1989.

McIntyre, Loren. *The Incredible Incas and Their Timeless Land*. Washington, D.C.: National Geographic Society, 1975.

Miller, Mary, and Karl Taube. *The Gods and Symbols of Ancient Mexico and the Maya: An Illustrated Dictionary of Mesoamerican Religion*. London: Thames and Hudson, 1993.

Morley, Sylvanus G., and George W. Brainerd. *The Ancient Maya*. 4th ed. Stanford, Calif.: Stanford University Press, 1983.

Moseley, Michael E. *The Incas and Their Ancestors*. New York: Harry N. Abrams, 1992.

Nicholson, Irene. *Mexican and Central American Mythology*. London: Paul Hamlyn Publishers, 1967.

Paden, R.C. *The Hummingbird and the Hawk*. New York: Harper and Row, 1967.

Peters, Daniel. *The Incas: A Magical Epic About a Lost World*. New York: Random House, 1991.

_____. *The Luck of Huemac: A Novel About the Aztec World*. New York: Random House, 1981.

_____. *Tikal: A Novel About the Maya World*. New York: Random House, 1983.

Sabloff, Jeremy A. *The New Archaeology and the Ancient Maya*. New York: W.H. Freeman Publishers, 1990.

Schele, Linda, and Mary E. Miller. *The Blood of Kings: Dynasty and Ritual in Maya Art*. London: Brazilier Press, 1992.

Schobinger, Juan. *First Americans*. Grand Rapids, Minn.: William E. Eerdmans Publishers, 1994.

Tedlock, Dennis, trans. *The Mayan Book of the Dawn of Life*. New York: Simon & Schuster, 1985.

Townsend, Richard. *The Aztecs*. New York: Thames and Hudson, 1992.

Von Hagen, Victor W. *Realm of the Incas*. New York: Mentor Books, 1961.

_____. *World of the Maya*. New York: Mentor Books, 1960.

Wauchope, Robert, ed. *The Indian Background of Latin American History: The Maya, Aztec, Inca and Their Predecessors*. Ann Arbor, Mich.: University of Michigan Press, 1970.

INDEX